A Friendly Guide to

Women in the Old Testament

Janina Hiebel

garratt
PUBLISHING

CONTENTS

INTRODUCTION 3

IN THE BEGINNING 9
- Eve, the first woman 10
- The Man and the Woman 10
- The serpent and the fruit 11
- Eve and her sons 12

THE FOUNDING MOTHERS 13
- Sarai/Sarah and Hagar 14
- Rebekah 15
- Leah, Rachel, Bilhah and Zilpah 17

WOMEN OF THE EXODUS 18
- Shiphrah and Puah 19
- Jochebed 19
- Pharaoh's daughter 20
- Miriam 20
- Zipporah 21
- Rahab 22

WOMEN IN THE BOOK OF JUDGES 23
- Deborah 24
- Jael 24
- Delilah 26

VICTIMS OF VIOLENCE 28
- Dinah 29
- Tamar 29
- Susanna 30

WOMEN AT THE DAWN OF THE MONARCHY 31
- Ruth and Naomi 32
- Hannah 35

FAMOUS QUEENS 38
- Michal 39
- Abigail 39
- Bathsheba 40
- The Queen of Sheba 41
- Jezebel 42
- Athaliah 43

WOMEN AND PROPHETS 44
- The widow of Zarephath 45
- The great woman of Shunem 46
- Huldah 46
- Gomer 47

SYMBOLIC WOMEN 48
- Daughter Zion 49
- Lady Wisdom 49
- Woman Strange 52
- The woman of strength 52

WOMEN HEROES 53
- Esther 54
- Judith 56

THEIR STORIES AND THEIR WISDOM FOR TODAY 59

MORE WOMEN IN THE OLD TESTAMENT 60

BIBLIOGRAPHY 62

ENDNOTES 63

ACKNOWLEDGMENTS 64

Cover image: Queen Esther by Andrea del Castagno c 1450 in Galleria degli Uffizi, Florence
Opposite page: threshing wheat in the traditional style

INTRODUCTION

Much of the Old Testament is written from a male perspective. This does not mean, however, that women characters are non-existent or irrelevant: women are as significant as men in bringing about God's plans – or in hindering them. Highlighting the female protagonists of Old Testament stories clarifies that the Bible is not just about men. We would seriously diminish salvation history if we reduced it to an affair between God and a handful of men. God's involvement with humanity concerns women and men together.

The Old Testament uses rich imagery when speaking of God, and includes female aspects that we can only understand if we notice biblical women and their social and religious roles. Some poetic texts portray God as a mother bird protecting her young (Deut 32:10–12; Ps 36:7, 61:4) or as a human mother consoling, teaching and feeding her children (Isa 66:13; Hos 11:3–4). God even makes clothes, a woman's job (Gen 3:21).

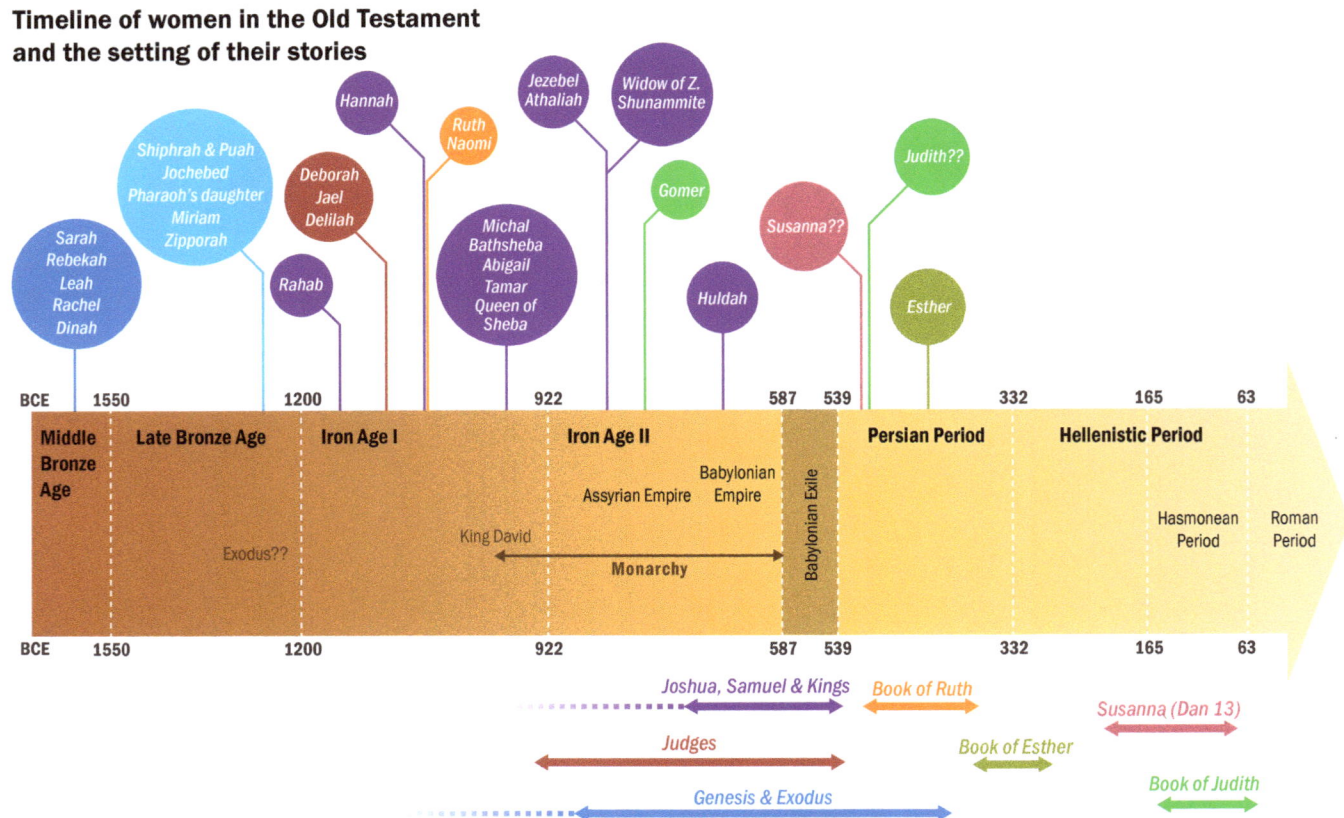

Timeline of women in the Old Testament and the setting of their stories

Timeline of Old Testament books and the writing of their stories

> Women's tasks typically included seasonal harvesting, health care and household management, fetching water, the production of food, textiles and various utensils, as well as the bearing and raising of children.

Despite the male bias of the scribes, in the Hebrew Bible, 'women are nowhere portrayed as less intelligent or capable than men; rather, they often appear as clever, competent, and sometimes heroic figures.'[a] In this book, we will encounter some of the women in the Old Testament. However we rarely meet ordinary women; everyday people, especially everyday women, rarely have their stories preserved. Their stories are told because they are the wife or the mother of someone famous, because they are queens, heroes, or because they are the victims of some heinous crime. In short, they are exceptional women.

Everyday life

Life in ancient Israel was very different from the individualistic, high-tech societies of today's developed world. To help us reflect on texts about women in the Old Testament, the following shows what life for ordinary women was like.

Most Israelites lived in an agrarian setting, in small hamlets, villages or fortified but very small towns. Cities contained a very small portion of the population, and only from about the eighth century onwards. City dwellers still worked in agriculture but some also did paid work. City life offered a market economy, including international trade.

Household, house and land

A typical household in rural Iron Age Israel included a complex family group: a senior couple, their unmarried children, and their married sons, and their wives and children. Wealthy households also had servants. Households were patrilocal: married sons generally stayed with their parents while daughters moved out to live with their husbands' families.

The most important asset of a household was its land. Their entire livelihood depended on the small terraced fields in a hilly, dry landscape. Land was passed down from father to son (patrilineal inheritance), making it vital to have at least one son. Having children was essential to meet the high labour demand of daily life. Married sons' wives ensured aged care for elderly parents.

Survival required hard work from every family member. Food shortages and malnutrition were common, as were infectious diseases. Men tended the fields, growing a variety of crops (mainly wheat, barley, legumes, vines, and olives), which depended heavily on seasonal rainfall. At harvest time everyone helped in the fields. Small flocks of sheep and goats were kept on the steeper

Opposite: remains of house at Horvat Haluquim

Above: textile production

hillsides, providing wool, and milk that was made into cheese. Meat was a rare treat reserved for festivals and special occasions. Vegetable gardens supplemented the diet with onions, cucumbers and herbs.

The so-called 'four-room house' was typical during the Iron Age. The ground level was built of stone. Stone pillars divided the front part of the house lengthwise into three rooms, with a fourth room across at the rear, where storage vessels were kept. The central front room was where the household mainly lived and worked. Most houses had a partial second story, and the flat roof (accessed by ladder) was also used for working and sleeping during the summer months. The paved side rooms could be used as stables during winter. People slept on mats that were stored away during the day. Some households lived in one house, others had a compound of several houses with a shared courtyard.

A woman's work

Women's tasks typically included seasonal harvesting, health care and household management, fetching water, the production of food, textiles and various utensils, as well as the bearing and raising of children. All of these responsibilities were crucial to the household's survival – no less important than the men's tasks.

The main staple food was bread. Women spent several hours each day grinding, kneading and baking to transform raw wheat or barley into flour and then bread. Food preparation also involved cooking lentils and vegetables, drying fruit such as grapes and figs, processing milk into cheese, and brewing beer.

Similarly, making a piece of clothing out of a heap of wool would take many hours of spinning and weaving. Standard clothing for both men and women included a long woollen tunic, held together at the waist by a belt or sash. Men wore a kind of mantle on top; women wore a large piece of fabric covering the back of their head and reaching down to the hem of the tunic. Clothing reflected one's marital and social status: linen was used mainly by the upper classes, whose clothing was more elaborate.

Women often shared time-consuming chores requiring more than one pair of hands, and some equipment (such as ovens) was communal. This collaboration was an opportunity for communication and created a network of solidarity and mutual assistance.

Women are mentioned in the Old Testament in professional roles – cooks and bakers at court, specialist textile producers and traders, businesswomen, prostitutes, midwives, professional mourners and prophets. But formal leadership positions outside the household were normally reserved for men.

Marriage

Contrary to our contemporary idea of marriage as the choice of two individuals, ancient Israelites understood marriage as the union of two families. In general, they saw themselves primarily as members of a group and only secondarily as individuals. Their personal wellbeing was inseparable from that of their group. The way we think about life choices of career, partner or housing would never have occurred to any ancient Near Eastern person. Most men and women had no choice in any of these matters.

Girls probably married in their mid-teens. Marriage was arranged by the fathers or senior male relatives of the bride and groom. Especially with wealthier families, a marriage contract detailed property arrangements. The groom's family acquired the right to marry her by paying a bride price in money, kind or labour to the bride's family.

The marriage became effective when the bride went to live with the groom in his father's house. Depending on the families' means, wedding celebration could extend over a week. The bride brought her dowry with her, including gifts from her family, her wedding outfit, and jewellery, all of which remained her property.

While men could marry more than one wife, most marriages were monogamous. Having many wives, and therefore many children, was a status symbol of kings in particular. Because children, especially sons, were so important, marrying a second wife became an attractive offer when a first marriage failed to produce offspring. In this case, the husband was not allowed to 'diminish the food, clothing, or marital rights of the first wife' (Exod 21:10).

However, according to Deut 24:1, a man could simply divorce his wife if he found 'something objectionable about her'. But a wife could not divorce her husband. Children remained with the family of their father.

Mothers and Children

Apart from their daily work, a major part of a woman's life included pregnancies, childbirth and child-rearing. Infertility posed an existential threat to a family, especially to a woman: childless women faced public shame and marginalisation, and risked divorce and destitution. Childlessness jeopardised the continuity of the family lineage and the couple's own aged care.

It was not uncommon for women to die in childbirth from complications, haemorrhage or

> ... in the Hebrew Bible, 'women are nowhere portrayed as less intelligent or capable than men; rather, they often appear as clever, competent, and sometimes heroic'

infections and the death rate of newborns was high. Some estimate an infant mortality rate of around 50%. Many more children died of disease before the age of five. This meant that women had to undergo many pregnancies to have any children survive into adulthood.

In the Hebrew Bible, women more often than men gave a name to their newborn. Women were the primary caregivers and educators for young children. Education essentially meant learning on the job, the transmission of knowledge and skills from one generation to the next. Children started helping with chores when they were very young. From the age of about six, girls helped their mothers with spinning, kneading, fetching water, looking after younger siblings, and tending to the vegetable garden; later on they learnt grinding, weaving, making pottery and more complex skills. Similarly, fathers taught their sons agricultural work, animal husbandry and other specialised skills. Flocks were tended by both boys and girls.

Mothers continued to be figures of authority for daughters and sons throughout their lives. Older women, respected for their wisdom and experience, would pass on traditions, cultural values and folktales to the young generation.

Below: A Judean family being deported during the Assyrian invasion in 701 BCE

Next page: spindle whorls from Jordan Museum and grinding stones

WOMEN IN THE OLD TESTAMENT

The following chapters show a selection of Old Testament women – mothers, sisters, wives, heroes, victims, and villains. We encounter them as literary characters in various stories and poems. Some of these women are more or less based on a historical person; there are some who are openly fictional or symbolic. Each of these women can be a mirror, a model, a warning, an inspiration, a teacher, an enemy, a friend, or all of the above.

This book does not discuss all the women in the Old Testament, but offers a first introduction, hoping to leave you wanting more.

Spindle Whorls

Made of bone, stone or pottery. Circular or spherical in shape with perforation in the middle where the spindle or rod was fitted in. The whorl, acting like a flywheel adds momentum to the spindle, and assists in increasing the spindle weight and extending the fiber to produce threads.

Iron Age II (1000-539 BC)
Tal Zar'a, Tal ar-Rumayth, Tal...
Tal Dayr 'Al...

IN THE BEGINNING

The book of Genesis narrates two different creation stories: In the seven-day creation account in Genesis 1:1–2:4a, an indefinite number of female and male human beings are created simultaneously. Men and women together are made in the image of God (1:27), are blessed, and are placed as stewards over all other creatures (1:28).

The second, but probably older account is the Garden of Eden tale (Gen 2:4b–3:24) and its sequel, the story of Cain and Abel (Gen 4). Only in this account, the first man and the first woman are individual characters, eventually named 'Adam' and 'Eve'.

EVE, THE FIRST WOMAN

Eve is not simply one woman in the Hebrew Bible: she is 'the Woman'. For most of the Garden of Eden tale, neither 'the man' nor 'the woman' has a personal name. They don't need names: there is only one man and one woman. Not until Gen 3:20 is the woman named *Eve* (similar to the Hebrew word for 'life'); *Adam* (meaning man, or human being) is not used as a name until Gen 4:25. The Woman and the Man represent *all* men and women, even though the way they are portrayed draws on men and women who were alive when the story was composed.

Ancient creation accounts are not guided by scientific interest (*when? where? how?*) but by the desire to explain aspects of life and its hardships (*why?*). Genesis 2–3 is no exception. It tells a story that is meant to explain the human condition: Why do we have to die? Why is life hard? Why are men and women attracted to each other, despite so much tension between them?

THE MAN AND THE WOMAN (GEN 2:7–25)

Different from the seven-day creation account in Gen 1:1 – 2:4a, the Garden Tale (Gen 2:4b – 3:24) narrates that God first forms 'a human/man' (*'adam*) from the soil and breathes life into him (2:7). God then plants a marvellous garden and entrusts it to the care of the human/man.

Eve's Creation

Eve, the Woman, is created in a unique way. Every other creature in Genesis 2 – Man, animals and birds – is formed 'out of the ground.' Only Woman is formed by dividing an already existing creature into two (2:22). Seeing that 'it is not good that the man should be alone' God creates for him 'a helper as his partner' (2:18). All too often these verses were taken to justify the subordination of women to men. This is not the meaning of the text's language.

The Hebrew word (*'ezer*) 'helper' appears 22 times in the Hebrew Bible: twice in Genesis 2; four times it has military connotations, and sixteen times it refers to God, as in Psalm 121:2: 'My *help* comes from the LORD, who made heaven and earth.' This shows that 'helper' in Gen 2:18 does not mean an assistant, or a housemaid, but it signifies someone who is indispensable, strong and certainly not inferior. The following Hebrew word, rendered 'as his

partner', means something like 'equal to him' or 'on the same level as him.' We could say that God creates a much-needed partner, equal to man.

As for the way Woman is created, one biblical scholar writes: *Some people maintain that being fashioned from the rib of the man makes the woman derivative and, therefore, inferior to him. This biased interpretation forgets that the man was made from the ground, and this has never been seen as a sign of his inferiority to Earth.*[b] Man's creation from the ground symbolises the deep connection that many farmers and First Nations People have to the land that nourishes them. Woman's creation from man symbolises the deep connection human beings have to each other, and in particular the mutual attraction between men and women (2:24).

In what follows, the two humans are mainly referred to as 'the man' (*ha'adam*) and 'his wife' (or 'his woman': *'ishto*). While this shows a male perspective, the Woman is never portrayed as inferior to the Man.

Two Trees in the Garden

Woman and Man live in a magnificent garden. The garden of Eden is not a geographical place; it is a symbolic place of harmony and plenty. Man and Woman are tasked with looking after this garden, but there is water in abundance and food grows on trees: no mention of sowing, weeding, harvesting, digging, grinding, baking or other work that real-life people in Old Testament times had to do.

Man and Woman are carefree, have little work to do, and are unaware of their own vulnerability. Since they are not allowed to eat from the 'tree of the knowledge of good and evil' (2:16–17), they do not know good and evil. In Deut 1:39 and Isa 7:15–16, this is seen as characteristic of young children. At the same time, the human couple are not forbidden from eating of the tree of life (2:9). Death, an ever-present reality in antiquity, is not part of life in the garden.

In the beginning, therefore, the Woman is in equal partnership with the Man, in a place of abundance, harmony and life.

THE SERPENT AND THE FRUIT (Genesis 3)

One day, Eve meets the serpent, the most intelligent animal that God has created (3:1), an ambiguous character with questionable motives. It approaches the Woman and draws her attention to the forbidden tree. The Man is present, too, as we learn a few verses later (3:6). His silent consent makes him the Woman's partner in crime. However, it is her decision to eat of its fruit.

Eve after Genesis

Already in Late Antiquity, commentaries and artwork on Genesis 2–3 shift towards demonising the serpent and portraying the woman either as weak and gullible or as closely associated with evil. 'Knowledge' is interpreted as sexual knowledge and consequently the temptation scene acquires erotic innuendo. Already in the book of Ecclesiasticus (second century BCE), Eve is blamed for committing the first sin. Both in Rabbinic and in Christian interpretation, Eve is portrayed as the temptress responsible for man's sin as well as her own. Christian interpretation also started to hold Eve responsible for the 'Fall' from an original state of grace, a concept that comes from Greek philosophy and is absent from the Hebrew Bible. In the writings of St Augustine, the Fall is connected to the idea of 'original sin' perpetuated throughout humankind.

DID YOU KNOW?

- It wasn't an apple! Genesis only talks about a *fruit* without specifying what kind of fruit.
- The words 'sin' and 'fall' are not used in Genesis 3. The text simply narrates what the Woman, the Man and the serpent say and do.
- In both creation accounts, humans seem to be vegetarians at first.

Previous page 9: Adam and Eve eating the forbidden fruit in the Garden of Eden in the cathedral of Brussels

Opposite page: Adam and Eve in the garden of Eden by J P Wenzel

What Tempted Eve?

Eve has abundant food, companionship and a good life. What could possibly tempt her? The Woman considers that the tree could make her 'wise' (3:6), an adjective that in other contexts is translated as 'successful' or 'prosperous'. The Woman seeks wisdom and progress – a driving force behind many human ambitions. In addition, the serpent promises that by eating from that tree 'you will be like God'. The real temptation is about refusing to accept the limitations of human life.

Wanting to gain more knowledge and to transcend one's limits is not evil in itself. These desires can affect humankind for good or ill, depending on the aims and the means employed. Wanting more without limits, and crossing boundaries as an end in itself can have terrible consequences, as climate change, colonialism, crime, injustice and war amply demonstrate. Wanting more, Eve makes an unwise decision: she disobeys God's command and then shares the forbidden fruit – and the responsibility of this – with her husband.

Consequences

The first thing the Woman and the Man *know* after eating the fruit is that they are naked. They are suddenly self-conscious and aware of how vulnerable they are. They hastily fashion leaf skirts to try to protect themselves.

Next, they realise that they have done something wrong, something irrevocable. Trust has been breached: God's trust in human beings, and Woman's and Man's trust in each other. The blame game that both engage in when confronted by God (3:12–13) shows this eloquently.

> **Eve has abundant food, companionship and a good life. What could possibly tempt her?**

Genesis 3:14–19 outlines the world Eve and her husband are going to live in from now on: a world similar to Israelite agrarian communities. God's sanctions affect the relationships of all parties involved: serpents and humans are now a threat to each other; the harmony between women and men is no longer a given; women will bring forth new life at great personal risk; men will harvest food only through back-breaking work. Their punishment is not immediate death, as originally threatened (2:17). However, death enters their world as Man and Woman are banished from the garden and lose access to the tree of life.

The Woman is now called Eve 'because she was the mother of all living' (3:20). Her name shows that life will continue. Eve's new life outside Eden includes motherhood as an integral part of it. She now becomes the prototype of 'the Mother' as well as the Woman.

EVE AND HER SONS (Genesis 4)

Eve and her husband raise two sons. When the boys grow up, Eve faces a new hardship. When Cain kills Abel, Eve loses both her sons: one to death, the other one because he is banished to 'be a fugitive and a wanderer' (4:14). Eve thus knows the pain of all mothers who have lost a child, and of all women suffering from the effects of violence within their own families.

Adam and Eve eventually have another son, Seth (4:25). Life continues. By now, Eve, the Woman, 'the mother of all living,' has gained legitimate knowledge through the joys and sufferings of life. She has learned resilience, skills and courage, and will pass these on to her children and their children for all generations to come.

Below: The Creation of Eve by Andrea Pisano
Opposite page: Rebekah and her servants from Cathedral de Monreale

THE FOUNDING MOTHERS

A major theme in Genesis 12–50 is God's double promise made first to Abraham: 'I will make of you a great nation' (12:2), and, 'To your offspring I will give this land' (12:7). These two promises – which both seem impossible – set in motion a saga that extends over three generations. In various twists and turns the fulfilment of the promises sometimes seems to come closer, then moves out of reach again. By the beginning of the book of Exodus, Israel will be a numerous people; however, it will take the rest of the Pentateuch and the book of Joshua to see them finally take possession of the Promised Land.

These stories are set in the distant past and are based on oral traditions. They were written down centuries later, and arranged in one book a long time after that. Because of this, no-one knows if any of the narrated events or individuals are based on historical 'facts'. The book of Genesis is not about historical facts; the truths it conveys are about how God and human beings interact with each other, and about human nature in general.

Typically, ancient Near Eastern stories about legendary founders focus on men. Genesis, too, displays male bias; however, the matriarchs are given remarkably prominent positions alongside the patriarchs in every generation. While many women in the Old Testament remain nameless, all of the founding mothers are named, even the slave girls. The fulfilment of God's promises depends as much on the women as on their husbands, and sometimes more.

SARAI/SARAH AND HAGAR
(Gen 11:29 – 23:19)

The name Sarai (or Sarah, as she is called from Gen 17:15 onwards) means 'Princess' and it says something about her character. Sarah is 'a woman beautiful in appearance' (12:11); a capable manager running the domestic affairs of a large and affluent semi-nomadic estate, a kind of travelling cattle station with sheep, goats and even camels.

Genesis says nothing about Sarah's background or family except that she marries Abraham in Ur of Mesopotamia (modern Iraq). Then the whole family migrates north to Haran (modern Turkey, close to the Syrian border). From there, Abraham and Sarai embark on the journey to Canaan.

The first thing we learn about Sarah is that she is 'barren' (11:30). Childlessness is a theme across the three generations of founding families and is particularly threatening in these stories. How can God make of Abraham 'a great nation' (12:2), when he and Sarah cannot have children?

Sarah faithfully follows her husband, courageously leaving her home and country behind twice. To protect Abraham, Sarah even lets herself be taken into some Pharaoh's harem during their stay in Egypt (12:10–20). God intervenes and has her restored to her husband – a sign that the promise of descendants applies to both Abraham and Sarah.

Hagar, Mother of Ishmael (Genesis 16–21)

Sarah's dominant personality shows in Genesis 16 when she gives her slave girl Hagar to Abraham as a concubine in order to 'obtain children by her' (16:2). Abraham merely plays along; he also leaves it up to Sarah how to treat Hagar afterwards. Hagar is Egyptian; although we are not told how she became Sarah's slave, she may have been one of the 'male and female slaves' given to Abraham by the abovementioned Pharaoh (12:16).

The use of servants as surrogate mothers appears as a common practice in Genesis, though a highly problematic one. Besides the moral issue of (ab)using a person in that way, we observe that it never solves the problem. Here, it creates additional conflict. As soon as Hagar knows that she is pregnant, she reclaims her dignity and begins to assert a position on a par with the lady of the house. Sarah retaliates. There are two parallel accounts of Hagar being driven into the desert: one during her pregnancy when she runs away from Sarah (16:6–14); and then, when her son Ishmael is still a child, Sarah has them expelled

> The book of Genesis is not about historical facts; the truths it conveys are about how God and human beings interact with each other, and about human nature in general.

Below: Map of the Middle East. It shows ancient cities and regions of different eras, as well as modern state borders.

permanently from the camp (21:8–21). Both times, Sarah is responsible for endangering Hagar's and Ishmael's lives. Both times, Abraham fails to defend them. Both times, an angel rescues mother and child. Ishmael receives his own promise from God. Hagar finds an Egyptian wife for her son and then disappears from view; no longer a slave, but still without a story of her own.

Sarah, Mother of Isaac

Sarah's attempt to force the promise has failed. God now explicitly announces, in Gen 17:16 and 18:10, that *Sarah* will be the mother of the promised heir. On both occasions, incredulous laughter is the response. After all, Sarah is 90 years old! Despite everything, nothing is 'too wonderful for the Lord' (18:14) and Sarah indeed gives birth to a son (21:2) who receives the fitting name Isaac: 'He-laughs'.

The promise finally seems within reach now – until God decides to put Abraham to the test. Sarah is not mentioned at all in the story of Isaac's almost-sacrifice (Genesis 22). Did she realise what was going on? Probably. Her trust in the ways of this mysterious God is tested as much as that of her husband. Sarah is not perfect – but then, neither is Abraham. If Abraham is called a 'model of faith' for following an impossible promise, Sarah equally deserves this title.

Sarah dies in Canaan at the age of 127 years (23:1–2). Her death, and therefore the need for a burial place, becomes the occasion for acquiring a first piece of land as permanent property: the beginning of the fulfilment of the second promise.

REBEKAH
(Gen 22:23 – 28:5)

Rebekah is the daughter of Bethuel, Abraham's nephew back in Haran. Her mother's name is not mentioned; her older brother Laban plays an important role later on.

Bride (Genesis 24)

After Sarah's death, Abraham sends an envoy to Haran with the mission of finding a 'proper wife' for Isaac from within the extended family. This is where we first encounter Rebekah, a teenage girl at a well. Rebekah is not only beautiful, she shows amazing hospitality as she generously offers to draw enough water to quench the thirst of ten camels. Clearly she is not afraid of hard work. As usual, the marriage is arranged among men: Abraham's servant and Rebekah's older brother. Rebekah is, however, the only woman in Genesis to be asked for her consent. Upon arrival in Canaan, Rebekah spots her future husband a mile away in the fields and runs to meet him (24:62–65). Isaac promptly falls in love with her (24:67).

Mother (Gen 25:20–34)

Rebekah, too, has difficulty having children. However, Rebekah's

Family tree of the descendants of Terah

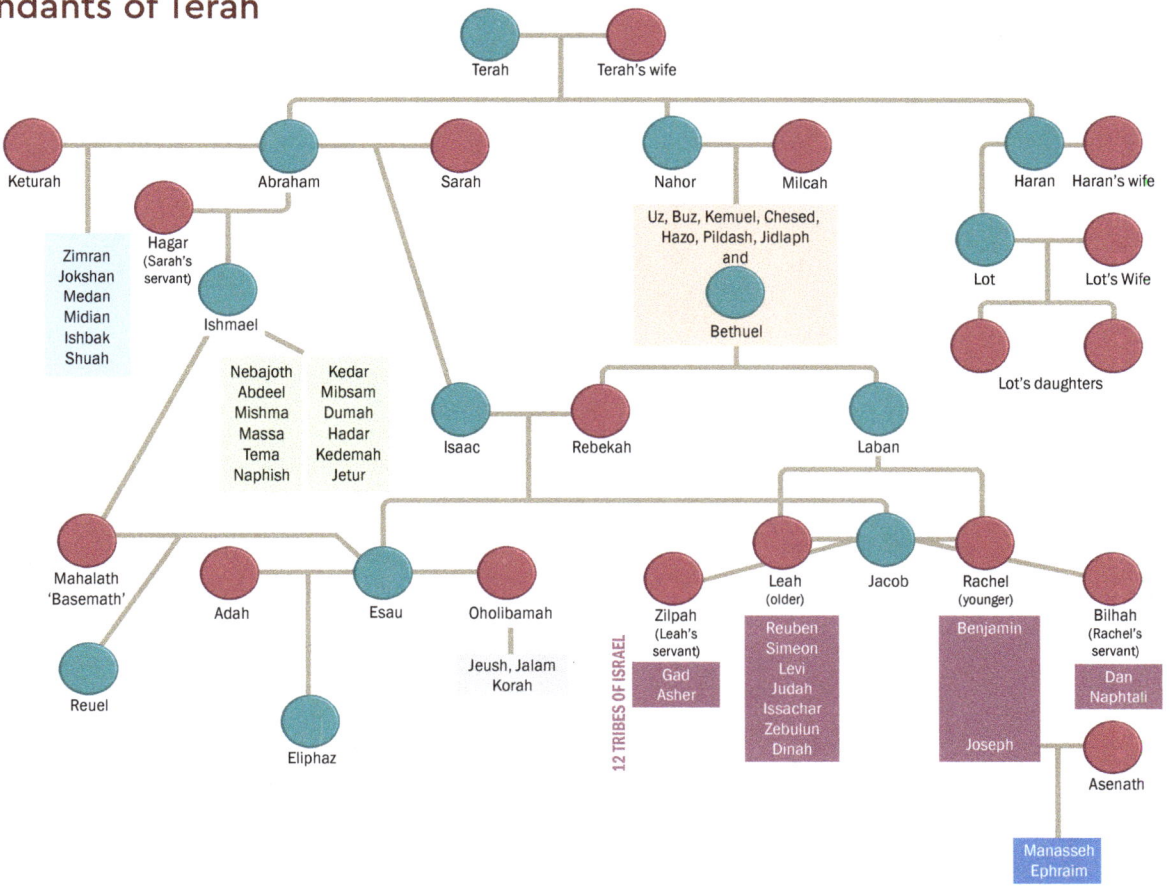

childlessness is overcome simply by Isaac's prayer (25:21). During her difficult pregnancy, Rebekah turns to God and receives a prophecy, stating that two nations will be born from her and that, contrary to tradition, the elder of her children will serve the younger (25:22–23).

Rebekah's twins are poles apart, both in appearance and in character. Isaac favours the firstborn, Esau, who is hairy and strong and becomes a skilled hunter, while Rebekah – probably with the divine oracle at the back of her mind – favours Jacob, who has smooth skin and inherited his mother's quick wits. The contrast between the brothers becomes most obvious in Gen 25:29–34 when Esau comes back hungry from an unsuccessful hunting trip. Jacob, who stayed at home cooking lentil stew, easily convinces Esau to give up his birthright (double share of inheritance) for a bowl of stew.

Trickster (Genesis 27)

Isaac, however, still favours Esau. Now blind and frail, Isaac plans to bestow his special paternal blessing on Esau alone – this would give Esau a position of superiority and make him the heir of God's promise to Abraham. Rebekah overhears the conversation, including that Esau is to bring his father a meal of freshly hunted game before receiving the blessing. Probably Rebekah has seen this coming for a while. Perhaps she and Isaac even argued about it. Now she will make sure that Isaac's paternal blessing will go to Jacob and not to Esau. Isaac cannot see. Can he be tricked into blessing Jacob by mistake? Rebekah quickly prepares a meal, dresses Jacob in Esau's clothes and covers his arms and neck with goat's hair. Isaac is deceived by the hairy feel and the smell of Esau's clothes, and he blesses Jacob. The episode shows who is really in charge in Isaac's tent, but portrays Rebekah in a morally ambiguous light.

To protect Jacob from Esau's anger,

Rebekah has him sent to her brother Laban. We presume her dead by the time Jacob returns; Rebekah never sees Jacob live out the blessing she made him 'steal' from his father. She never sees him settle down and have a family that will continue God's promise to Abraham, whose heir he is now.

LEAH, RACHEL, BILHAH AND ZILPAH (Gen 29–31; 35:16–20)

Rachel's first appearance seems straight out of a Hollywood love story: a young woman leads her father's sheep to a well where a handsome stranger single-handedly rolls away the huge stone covering the well and gallantly proceeds to water the sheep for her. They immediately fall in love, or at least Jacob does. However, although Jacob and Rachel do get married, they do not live 'happily ever after'.

Marriage fraud

Rachel is the younger daughter of Laban, Rebekah's brother. Her older sister is Leah. There is no mention of their mother. Rachel is pretty and used to getting what she wants. Leah is not described as pretty but she has 'tender eyes', perhaps meaning that she is kind, though the adjective has a nuance of vulnerability as well. It is easy to imagine her growing up in the shadow of her charming younger sister.

Their father is a ruthless businessman, always looking for ways to make a profit. Jacob agrees to work for Laban for seven years, since he has no means to pay the bride price for Rachel. He proves himself useful with the flocks, so Laban decides to keep him – by tricking him into marrying Leah instead of Rachel. As the bride remains heavily veiled during the wedding day, Jacob only realises the morning after that he has married the wrong sister. His open dismay at this discovery would have been hurtful for Leah, even shameful. Perhaps Leah tried to convince herself that Jacob would eventually come to love her, but Jacob only has eyes for Rachel. He immediately renegotiates to marry Rachel as well – for seven more years of work.

The only one who is sympathetic to Leah in this story is God. 'When the Lord saw that Leah was unloved, he opened her womb; but Rachel was barren' (29:31). This is the first time God is mentioned in Leah's and Rachel's story. Again, God is on the side of the weaker party.

Bilhah, Rachel's servant, and Zilpah, Leah's servant

Rachel first reacts to her situation with resentment, blaming Jacob (30:1). Then she resorts to the same strategy as Sarah: she uses her servant girl Bilhah as a surrogate mother. Bilhah is only seen as a means to an end; her wishes don't matter. She was given to Rachel as part of her dowry, then given to Jacob so that Rachel could have a child. Later she is taken by Leah's eldest son Reuben, who sleeps with her to defy his father.

Bilhah gives birth to two sons. The competition between the two sisters continues as Leah in turn sends her maid Zilpah to Jacob, to have more children through her. Zilpah also has two sons.

Sisterly rivalry continues

In an almost comical scene, Leah and Rachel bargain over some mandrakes. Mandrake roots were believed to have fertility-assisting properties. Rachel wants them. She 'barters' Jacob for the night in exchange, which is doubly ironic: first, because throughout this story, it is the women who decide who Jacob spends the night with – he seems to have no more say in the matter than do Bilhah and Zilpah. Second, although Rachel gets the mandrakes, it is Leah who conceives that night – because 'God heeded Leah' (30:17).

Only after Leah has had seven children (a perfect number), 'God remembered Rachel' (30:22) and she, too, has a son. While she seems grateful, she immediately asks for more: 'she named him Joseph, saying "May the Lord add to me another son!"' (30:24).

Rachel gets what she wanted. But she tragically dies giving birth to her second son, Benjamin, and is buried along the way. The unremarkable and unloved Leah, on the other hand, becomes the ancestress of Israel's kings and priests, and is buried in the family plot with Abraham, Sarah, Isaac and Rebekah. Both Leah and Rachel were unhappy, and so, we assume, were their maids Bilhah and Zilpah. Each of their stories is, in different ways, fraught with injustice. Despite their differences, the four women are forever bound together as the mothers of Israel's twelve tribes; the matriarchs of the chosen people of God's covenant with Abraham.

Opposite page: Rebekah (detail), from St Patrick's church, Coleraine, Ireland

DID YOU KNOW?

- The book of Genesis was not written in one go. There are various theories, but many scholars assume that there were two or three independent sources that were woven together only later. This would explain why there are contradictions, why some stories seem to be told twice with minor variations, and why the individual episodes are not always in chronological order.

- Most major characters in the book of Genesis have exaggerated age spans that make Sarah's 127 years appear quite young. These numbers are not meant to be taken literally. They reflect the idea that great age is a blessing from God and so they are one way of expressing just how much Abraham and Sarah were blessed.

WOMEN OF THE EXODUS

The story of how God freed the Israelites from Egyptian oppression and led them through the wilderness to the Promised Land has inspired readers and artists of different times, places and cultures for centuries. While some details in the story place the Exodus events sometime in the Late Bronze Age (maybe in the 1200s), there is no evidence of them, or of the military conquest of Canaan, anywhere outside the Bible. Despite the lack of historical confirmation, this is still a powerful tale of liberation and transformation.

As usual, the main characters of the Exodus story are male, but women figure throughout the storyline. Women have vital roles in the life of Moses; a woman is co-leader of the Israelites as they venture into the wilderness, and a woman is instrumental to their arrival in the Promised Land. Without the women, the Exodus could not have happened.

SHIPHRAH AND PUAH (Exod 1:15–21)

It begins like a fairy tale: a wicked monarch attempts to kill newborn babies that he sees as a threat. Like a fairy tale, no year is specified and the evil king does not have a name. In Exodus 1, 'Pharaoh' attempts the genocide of the Hebrew population under his dominion by ordering the Hebrew midwives to kill all their male newborns. Unlike mighty Pharaoh, the two humble midwives have names: Shiphrah and Puah – one of the many ironies in this chapter. The contrast between two apparently powerless women and the powerful Pharaoh could not be greater. In ancient Egyptian culture, a Pharaoh is more than a human being: he embodies the divine world order, a presence of the god Horus. Pharaoh claims divine authority but is not upholding justice, as is his duty. Shiphrah and Puah simply ignore Pharaoh's command because they revere the God of life, not him. Quietly they continue their work, doing their duty, thereby saving Israel from destruction. Pharaoh's plan fails because of two women who follow their consciences and refuse to follow orders. The civil disobedience of Shiphrah and Puah stands for countless brave women and men throughout history who did not surrender their consciences to inhumane regimes.

JOCHEBED (Exod 2:1–10)

All we are initially told about the mother of Moses is that she is of the tribe of Levi (2:1). Only Exod 6:20, the genealogy of Moses, includes her name: Jochebed.

Jochebed faces a mother's worst nightmare: losing her child. Rational reasoning would have told her that leaving a three-months-old baby in a basket on the river is perilous; but Jochebed is buying time, desperately hoping for a miracle. How many mothers around the world and across the centuries have taken desperate risks in the hope of saving their child from danger? These mothers do not always receive the miracle they need.

Opposite page: Bas-relief of Miriam by A V Loganovsky on the cathedral of Christ the Saviour, Donskoy Monastery, Moscow

Below: Map of the area relevant to the Exodus story, including ancient trade routes.

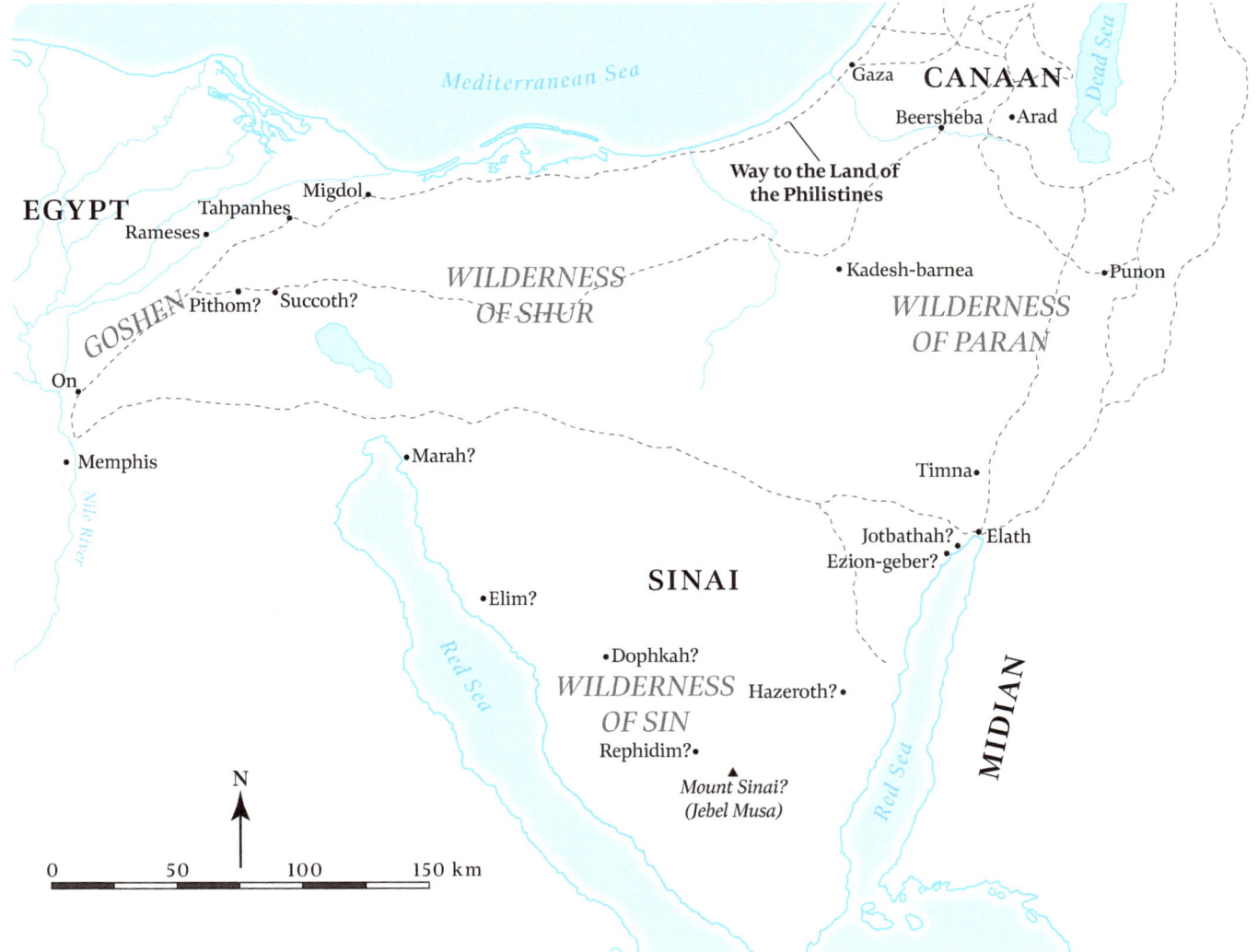

But for Moses' mother, it happens: her child survives, she can hold him in her arms again – she is even paid to nurse him (2:9).

PHARAOH'S DAUGHTER
(Exod 2:5–10)

The person responsible for this miracle is the daughter of the very Pharaoh who wanted the child dead. Like her father, she remains without a name. Unlike her father, she shows human decency. Pharaoh's daughter understands that the crying baby boy in the basket is one of the Hebrew children (2:6). But her reaction is compassionate, guided by motherly instincts, not by political ideologies. We are not told what this young woman thought of her father's harsh policies; her story highlights only this moment of human kindness that leads her to save the boy. The nameless daughter of the nameless Pharaoh is the only positive Egyptian character in the book of Exodus.

MIRIAM
(Exod 2:4–8; 15:20–21; Numbers 12)

At this point, the boy's older sister appears on the scene. She is referred to as 'young woman' (2:8), so she must be in her early teens. Though nameless in this chapter, she is vital to its successful outcome, as she courageously addresses Pharaoh's daughter, offers to find a nurse for the baby and thus enables the decision that reunites mother and son. The actions of all three women together – mother, sister and Pharaoh's daughter – ensure the survival of this one Hebrew boy who will become the hero and main character of what follows. Where women collaborate for the good, life and hope are hard to extinguish.

Later in the book of Exodus we are told that Moses had an older brother, Aaron (6:20) who had a sister, Miriam (15:20). The first time Miriam is

> Pharaoh's plan fails because of two women who follow their consciences and refuse to follow orders.

Below: Miriam and Israelite women dancing, 14th century Catalonia

explicitly called Moses' sister is in the book of Numbers (Num 26:56; also 1 Chron 6:3). It is unclear if the sister in Exodus 2 is the same person as Miriam in the later chapters.

When Miriam is first introduced by name she is called 'the prophet Miriam, Aaron's sister'. After the crossing of the Sea of Reeds (Exodus 14), Miriam sings, leading 'all the women … with tambourines and with dancing' (15:20). Miriam's song consists of one verse and is the oldest existing account of the Exodus.

> *Sing to the LORD, for he has triumphed gloriously;*
> *horse and rider he has thrown into the sea (15:21).*

Her song echoes the song of Moses in 15:1–18 (or vice-versa). From the shores of the sea, the trio of Moses, Miriam and Aaron lead their people into the wilderness towards freedom.

Miriam appears again in a startling incident in the book of Numbers, chapter 12. Aaron and Miriam are reproached by God for challenging Moses's special status as a prophet. Aaron gets away with cautioning but Miriam is struck by a skin disease, which leads to her being excluded from the camp for seven days. While this seems unfair, the importance of Miriam to the community is highlighted by the fact that no one leaves until she returns.

Like Aaron and Moses, Miriam dies en route to the Promised Land (Num 20:1). None of the three leaders reach the land towards which they have been guiding their people. Miriam was remembered as a leader, as we see in the words of the prophet Micah: 'For I brought you up from the land of Egypt, and redeemed you from the house of slavery; and I sent before you Moses, Aaron, and Miriam' (Mic 6:4).

ZIPPORAH (Exod 2:15–22; 4:24–26)

Moses and Zipporah meet during Moses' exile in Midian, in the north-western part of the Arabian Peninsula (2:15–22). Like Jacob and Rachel, they meet at a well where Moses defends Zipporah and her six sisters against some aggressive shepherds. The women's father, a Midianite priest, then invites Moses to stay. Moses is welcomed into the

Below: Moses and his Ethiopian wife, identified in some traditions with Zipporah, Jacob Jordaens, 1593—1678

Opposite page: Drummers, pottery 8th-7th century BCE, Israel Museum

Below: Miriam from the windows of St Pierre-le-Jeune, Strasbourg

family and marries Zipporah. The couple settles in Zipporah's father's household and they soon have a son.

Their peaceful family life is shaken up by Moses's encounter with God at the burning bush. Moses and Zipporah pack their sons and belongings onto a donkey (they have had another baby) and return to Egypt. Whatever Zipporah might think of her husband's decision, she understands that reconnecting with his kin is important to him. One night during their journey, without warning, God 'tried to kill him' (4:24). It is not clear whether God is threatening Moses, or his first-born son, or what form the attack takes. Biblical scholars think that the incident may be symbolic, foreshadowing the Passover, the tenth plague, or the general seriousness of what lies ahead.c In any case, the person who saves Moses (and/or his son) is again a woman: this time, his wife. Zipporah acts quickly. Instead of providing conventional first aid, she performs the ritual of circumcision (which is normally done only by men). At this, God withdraws and the Exodus story can continue.

Moses sends Zipporah and their two sons back to her father at some stage (18:2–3). The four of them visit Moses when the Israelites pass through Midian (18:6), but, perhaps surprisingly, they do not stay long. On the level of the story's theological agenda, it ensures that no non-Israelites are present at the Covenant at Mount Sinai (Exodus 24).

The midwives, Jochebed, Pharaoh's daughter, and Zipporah are women who see what is needed and do what they can. They collaborate with God in an enterprise of deliverance and liberation far greater than they could imagine.

RAHAB (Josh 2:1–21; 6:22–25)

If Shiphrah and Puah stand at the prologue to the Exodus story, Rahab is a vital part of its completion: the arrival in the Promised Land. The story reads like an espionage thriller: two Israelite spies arrive in Jericho and lodge at a place that may be an inn, or a brothel, or both. The king of Jericho has already received intel of their whereabouts, so their life is in danger. Enter Rahab, the owner of the place, a Canaanite woman with no husband and questionable morals. Like Pharaoh's daughter, she is an unlikely ally. Like the midwives, she resists orders. Rahab hides the two men on the flat rooftop and sends the king's guards in the wrong direction. A strategic planner as well as a clever businesswoman, Rahab has a deal in mind. She foresees the fall of Jericho and all Canaan because she recognises the power of Israel's God. As she protects the spies, she asks for protection in return: for herself, her parents and her siblings. In doing so, Rahab does not simply defect to the side of the winners. She acts with *hesed* (kindness, faithful love, loyalty) not only towards her birth family but towards the Israelite God and the Israelite people, and the spies promise her the same in return (Josh 2:12–14). Her help is not just a business investment but motivated by deeper sentiments; the New Testament Letter to the Hebrews credits her with 'faith' (Heb 11:31; see Jam 2:25).

When Jericho falls, the Israelites honour the bargain (Josh 6:22–25): Rahab and her relatives are safe. The fall of Jericho is the beginning of what the book of Joshua narrates as the conquest of Canaan – not so much by the Israelite army but by the Israelite God. Rahab's intuition was spot-on. The foreign woman of dubious reputation teaches all Bible readers about recognising God's greatness and choosing to side with God's plans.

> The foreign woman of dubious reputation teaches all Bible readers about recognising God's greatness and choosing to side with God's plans.

WOMEN IN THE BOOK OF JUDGES

The book of Judges is set during Iron Age I (1200-922 BCE), before Israel's monarchy was established. It tells stories of heroic military leaders who save the tribes of Israel from oppression by surrounding nations.

Most of these heroes are men. This chapter is about three women whose actions dramatically change the military situation of their time: Israel's only female judge and leader, and two foreign women who may be heroes or villains, depending on who is telling the story.

DEBORAH
(Judges 4–5)

Deborah is the only woman in this series of heroes and the only one whose story is told twice: once in prose (Judges 4) and again in poetry (Judges 5). The 'Song of Deborah' is one of the oldest texts in the Bible and it is likely that Deborah is a historical figure, with some legendary flair added.

Deborah is not introduced by way of male relatives. She is not 'Deborah, the daughter of x' or 'the mother of y'. It is not even sure if the phrase that is usually translated as 'wife of Lappidoth' (4:4) actually means that: it could also mean something like 'fiery woman'. Deborah is introduced on her own merits: as a prophet and a judge (4:4). In the course of Judges 4–5, Deborah is also portrayed as military leader, liberator and 'mother in Israel' (5:7), a title of honour implying a leadership role in protecting and advising the people of Israel.

We know nothing of Deborah's personal life, how old she was, or when and how she became such a prominent figure. Most likely she was married, probably had children – but the point is that the book of Judges focuses just on her and her leadership, without feeling the need to mention her family situation or her ancestry. She was so famous that, as with modern celebrities, everyone knew which 'Deborah' was being referred to.

Judge, prophet and leader

As a judge, Deborah holds office 'under the palm of Deborah' (4:5). People come to her to settle disputes or legal matters. She is a person of authority, renowned for her wisdom, her impartiality and her direct connection to God.

At the time the Israelites had been 'cruelly' oppressed for twenty years (4:3) by the Canaanite King Jabin and his powerful army led by the general Sisera. God responds to Israel's pleas for help through the prophet Deborah, revealing a plan for liberation. Like many everyday tasks of Iron Age women, that plan needs two pairs of hands, or rather, two leaders: a strategist and a military commander.

Deborah's leadership skills include the art of organising and delegating, so she sends for a man called Barak and tells him the plan. As Barak hesitates, Deborah promises to go into battle with him, but she also makes it clear that Barak will gain no glory, 'for the Lord will sell Sisera into the hand of a woman' (4:9).

Things work out exactly as Deborah predicted: As the Israelite soldiers assemble on Mt Tabor, Sisera moves his more powerful army against them. It is Deborah who decides the day of the battle and gives the go ahead. Aided by a torrential downpour, which renders Sisera's chariots useless, the Israelites have a smashing victory. Sisera, however, in disgraceful violation of his responsibilities as a general, escapes on foot.

JAEL
(Judg 4:17–22; 5:24–27)

Not even Deborah foresees the next turn of events – that there is a third partner in their alliance: Jael, a Midianite woman. Jael's people are nomads who live in tents. They are not at war with King Jabin.

Jael does something very unusual: she invites the fleeing Sisera into her tent. If her husband, the head of the clan, did this, it would be a gesture of hospitality. But for a woman, it is risky and scandalous to invite a stranger in – especially without her husband around. Usually after a battle, Sisera and his soldiers would have forcibly entered women's dwellings with harmful intentions. This time, Sisera is alone and scared for his life, seeking only protection. Jael seems caring and hospitable.

In reality, Jael is anything but hospitable. Perhaps she wants to ingratiate herself with the victorious Israelites. Perhaps Sisera's army has harmed other women around the area; perhaps she has her own score to settle. We know nothing about Jael's motives, only about her actions. Pitching and dismantling tents was women's work, so tent pegs and a hammer would have been quick at hand. As Sisera falls asleep (another dishonourable action for a general on duty), Jael drives a tent peg through his head. Then she waits outside until Barak arrives and she delivers the corpse.

Deborah's prophecy that 'the Lord will sell Sisera into the hand of a woman' (4:9) thus comes true. Jael may be a killer or a hero, or both; in any case she seals the victory. The poetic rendering of the story praises her as 'most blessed of women' (5:24). Victory is achieved by the (partly unwitting) collaboration of

---

DID YOU KNOW?

- 'Deborah' means 'Bee.' While we might think of busy bees and honey, in the Old Testament a swarm of bees can be a metaphor for an attacking army (see Deut 1:44; Isa 7:18; Ps 118:12).[d]

- Although most paintings depict Delilah with a pair of scissors, Judg 16:19 is ambiguous about who shaves Samson's hair: Delilah or the man she calls. The most common translations attribute this action to the man. Scissors are never mentioned.

Above: Fresco of Jael killing Sisera by Pietro Paolo Vasta, church of San Camillo, Acireale, Italy

GOD AND WAR

Old Testament texts often associate God with war. Contemporary readers feel justifiably uneasy about this. The terrible wars of the twentieth century and the current age have caused many to realise the evils of war, especially when religion is its justification. The shameful histories of the Crusades and other purportedly faith-inspired wars, horrify us.

Antiquity had a different perspective: localised wars between neighbouring groups or nations were common. There was no separation between public life and religion. Every public or political act was also religious, and vice versa. In a mainly polytheistic world, each nation had its own national deity, so wars between states were seen as a fight between their gods. Besides the size and skill of one's army, it was the power of one's god that determined the outcome. Biblical texts are steeped in this mentality, especially the book of Judges. In very old texts, like the Song of Deborah, God is portrayed as a warrior fighting alongside the Israelite army. Israel's victory is then God's victory. It is also important to remember that, over the centuries of biblical history, the 'God as warrior' tradition flourished especially in situations of oppression and defeat. It served to give hope and courage to underdogs, rarely to justify violence by the powerful. Only in later texts, after the Babylonian Exile, do we find the idea that Israel's God is the one universal God of all nations, and thus of peace.

two women and a man successfully liberating the Israelites from twenty years of oppression, reminding us that God's ways are unpredictable in using likely and unlikely allies.

DELILAH (JUDGES 16)

What would Jael's story look like if told from the Canaanite point of view? A comparable tale of a woman overcoming a warrior is the story of Samson and Delilah – only this time the warrior is Israelite. Samson, whose miraculous birth was announced to his mother by an angel (Judges 13), is a Hercules-type war hero. God has given him superhuman strength, but he is less gifted in social skills and common sense. When it comes to women, he is hopeless. His wedding with a Philistine woman results in annulment, thirty dead Philistines, a destroyed harvest and the entire family of his ex-bride burnt to death by the people of their own town (14:1–15:6).

No one can overcome Samson until 'he fell in love with a woman in the valley of Sorek, whose name was Delilah' (16:4). Delilah's nationality, family ties, or social status are not mentioned. The valley of Sorek lies between Israelite and Philistine territory, giving the possibility that Delilah is Philistine like Samson's wife but the text never specifies this. Delilah is simply herself: the only named woman in Samson's story, and the only person to master Samson's strength.

Just as Jael delivered the sought-after warrior Sisera to his enemies, Delilah delivers the sought-after warrior Samson to his enemies but with two differences: Delilah is paid a fortune to do this, whereas Jael acts out of her own initiative. Jael kills Sisera at what appears to be their first encounter, while Delilah is in a relationship with Samson and hands him over alive. After three failed attempts, Delilah succeeds in discovering the secret of Samson's strength: his hair. She promptly has his head shaved and Samson is captured, tortured and imprisoned. Delilah betrays the man who loves her but arrogantly thinks he is invincible. What became of Delilah afterwards? The story is silent about her future. From the Israelite point of view, Delilah is a villain and a traitor. But the Philistines may well have written a song about her.

Jael and Delilah remind us that perspective decides who is proclaimed a hero and who is called a traitor. Their stories record the influence their actions had on their people, but both women also had their own personal agendas. Deborah, on the other hand, is a prophet and military leader – a welcome challenge to stereotypes of women as weak or subordinate.

Below: Mt Tabor looking towards Nain

Opposite page: Statue of Delilah and Samson by Aliza Alon

VICTIMS OF VIOLENCE

While Jael and Delilah inflict violence on others, women in the Old Testament are frequently the victims of violence. Crimes of sexual violence against women occurred in biblical times, and are reflected in biblical texts. In biblical stories, violence against a woman always unleashes more violence. It is a serious crime that corrodes the social fabric, truly a 'thing that ought not to be done' (Gen 34:7). These texts have a limited, exclusively male perspective, often more concerned with restoration of honour than with safeguarding, justice and healing for victims.

The stories of the three women (all victims of sexual violence) in this sad chapter come from three different Old Testament books and are set in three different times. Dinah, Tamar and Susanna are not the only women in the Old Testament who suffer this fate; their stories stand for many others and for all human histories and cultures.

The stories of Dinah and Tamar differ in setting and detail but have much in common. Both are victims of rape before they are betrothed, which means they are very young, maybe in their early teens. In both cases, their father does nothing, despite holding a prominent position. Both Dinah and Tamar are avenged by older brothers who are driven by the need to restore the family's honour as well as genuine concern for their sister. Both times, the rapist pays with his life, and there are further casualties on a larger scale. But both Dinah and Tamar disappear from view; nothing is said about what became of them.

DINAH
(Genesis 34)

Dinah, the youngest of Leah's children, falls prey to a stranger – Shechem, son of a local chief – while outside her father's camp. As an unmarried girl, Dinah is relatively free in her movements, as were her grandmother Rebekah and her aunt Rachel at that age. But leaving the camp is Dinah's only autonomous action in this tragedy. After that, she is abducted, raped, bargained for, avenged and finally rescued. Nothing is written about her thoughts and feelings. Dinah is a victim, powerless to speak up or act for herself. In that, Dinah is similar to the many voiceless women, both ancient and modern, who are abused, held captive and without rights.

The crime committed against Dinah also affects her family, especially her male relatives, who had the responsibility of protecting her. While they have not been physically assaulted, their honour is damaged – something that Shechem and his father do not recognise when they come to negotiate a marriage. Only later we learn that they were holding Dinah hostage – shedding doubt on Shechem's assurance that he 'loves' her. But Dinah's father Jacob takes no action at all. Two of Dinah's older brothers, Simeon and Levi, use deceit to liberate Dinah and then kill not only Shechem but all the men in the settlement. Violence escalates further as Jacob's other sons join in and loot the place, taking goods and animals and 'all their little ones and their wives' (Gen 34:29) – showing that they are in no way morally superior to the Canaanites.

Dinah's traumatic experience is merely hinted at, as the men in this episode care mainly about matters of honour, tribal identity, and business. By the end of the chapter, many lives are devastated or lost, a town lies ruined, and Israelite-Canaanite relations are compromised. The limitation in this biblical text is the omission of a voice for Dinah, and for her sisters in every age.

TAMAR
(2 Samuel 13)

Tamar is the daughter of King David and Princess Maacah, roughly around the year 1000 BCE. As a yet-unbetrothed princess in the royal palace of Jerusalem, Tamar would have been heavily guarded, with much less freedom to move about than Dinah. She should have been safe, but she wasn't. It is not a stranger who assaults Tamar but her older half-brother Amnon, David's firstborn son, the crown prince. Amnon is obsessed with Tamar and concocts a plan to be alone with her. Tamar is sent for to prepare food for her supposedly ill brother, which she does willingly and unsuspectingly. When they are alone, Amnon tries to persuade Tamar to sleep with him, to which Tamar resolutely answers that 'such a thing is not done in Israel' (13:12). She reasons with him, pleads with him, even suggests that he could marry her if he only talked to their father – all to no avail. The story leaves no room for 'blaming the victim'; it sharply contrasts Tamar's innocent decency with the disgraceful behaviour of Amnon. Even after the rape, Tamar is still assertive, imploring him to stand by what he has done, which would mean marrying her. That Tamar even suggests this is only conceivable against the background of a group-oriented identity and the cultural value of honour. A marriage would restore their personal honour as well as that of the royal family. Amnon's response is to have her thrown out of his house. Her body and her dignity violated, Tamar tears her garment and puts ashes on her head, as though mourning. The type of dress she was wearing showed her status as a virgin princess and that status was indeed torn and gone. And Tamar cries, not quietly but aloud – but nobody listens.

Only Tamar's brother Absalom realises what happened and shelters Tamar in his household, 'a desolate woman' (13:20). When David fails to punish his firstborn, Absalom takes matters in his own hands. He has Amnon killed, flees, and spends three years in exile. The estrangement between David and Absalom later escalates into civil war, more killing and more rape. At the end of this

DID YOU KNOW?

- We do not know whether Dinah existed historically. What happens to her was, however, a realistic danger for girls and women throughout biblical times.

- Tamar may well have been a historical person, as at least some of the stories about David's reign are based on court records.

- 'Susanna' is a fictional short story, written between the third and first centuries BCE. It was added only to the Greek version of the book of Daniel. In some Bible editions, 'Susanna' is listed as a separate book with the so-called Apocrypha. The systemic injustice it portrays is likely realistic. Although Susanna is clearly an innocent victim, many paintings from the 16th century onwards perpetuate the injustice by portraying her as temptress.

story there are broken lives, broken relationships, political instability, war and death.

Tamar's story is inserted in the wider context of the beginnings of Israelite monarchy; it is part of a critical voice that points out the shortcomings and dangers of monarchy: if a king cannot protect his own daughter, how will he protect anyone in his kingdom?

SUSANNA
(Daniel 13)

Susanna's story is different and set many centuries later. Susanna is a married woman with children, the wife of an influential, wealthy man in Babylonia's Jewish community. Though saved from physical violence, Susanna is a victim of sexual harassment, attempted rape, and outrageous injustice.

Like Tamar, Susanna knows the men who prey upon her, but suspects nothing. Susanna has no idea that two of her husband's colleagues, elders of the community, have been nurturing indecent intentions towards her. They eventually conspire to catch her alone and use extortion: either Susanna submits to their lust or they will accuse her of adultery with a mystery man. Susanna realises that she is 'completely trapped' (v. 22) but she still has one choice that Dinah and Tamar did not have: Susanna can and does choose to resist the men, as her cries for help are sure to be heard.

What follows is like a courtroom drama. The legal situation is damning: According to Lev 20:10 and Deut 22:22, being caught in adultery is punishable by death for both parties. According to Deut 17:6; 19:15 and Num 35:30, any charge needs to be sustained by at least two witnesses. This enables the two elders to plot false charges, corroborate each other's testimony, and have Susanna condemned to death. They know that their position as elders and judges, along with the fact that they are two men against one woman, will preclude any thorough investigation. A classic case of conspiracy to pervert justice, with a sexist twist.

As she is sentenced to death, Susanna appeals to the highest-ranking judge of all: God. The answer to her prayer is young Daniel coming to the rescue, like brilliant lawyers in courtroom dramas. His separate cross-examination quickly reveals the perjury, and the two elders are condemned to the same death they wanted to inflict on Susanna. Susanna herself is acquitted and her reputation restored.

While this is intended as an edifying ending, it leaves a bitter taste: the system is still flawed, trust is still broken. The bystanders and judges hopefully have learned not to believe everything they are told. Susanna, too, has learned something: that despite her impeccable reputation, no-one (except a stranger) stood up for her when she really needed help. She risked death to remain faithful to her husband and to herself. Her husband did nothing to save her. Could their life ever be the same afterwards?

> **In biblical stories, violence against a woman always unleashes more violence. It is a serious crime that corrodes the social fabric, truly a 'thing that ought not to be done'**

Opposite page: Ruth and Naomi (detail) from window in Rodef Shalom Synagogue, Pittsburgh PA. Photo attributed to Danita Dellimont

WOMEN AT THE DAWN OF THE MONARCHY

This chapter is about three women who struggle with, and overcome, seemingly insurmountable difficulties: Ruth and Naomi face grief and poverty; Hannah faces bullying and her inability to have a child.

Theirs are not simply stories of personal victories, however; their courage, resolve and devotion are also laying the foundations for the emergence of Israel as a nation just a few generations later.

RUTH AND NAOMI

Naomi and Ruth are migrants. Because of a severe drought in Bethlehem, Naomi's husband Elimelech decides to try his luck in Moab. There were no visas at the time, no border control; but settling into a new place was still hard – people didn't trust foreigners. Somehow Naomi and Elimelech manage. Their two sons marry lovely Moabite women, Orpah and Ruth.

One after the other, Naomi's husband and both her sons die. Naomi is left with her two daughters-in-law, without any income, protection, or extended family. Naomi only sees one solution: migrate again, back to Bethlehem. The famine there is over, and at least there may be family or old friends to call on.

'Where you go, I will go'

Ruth, one of Naomi's Moabite daughters-in-law, is determined to come with her. Widowed at a young age, Ruth could marry again and rebuild her life among her own people. Yet Ruth considers Naomi her family. Their relationship has grown strong over the years, even more so through the shared grief and sorrow. Driven by affection and loyalty, Ruth also becomes a migrant. Her words are famous:

> *Where you go, I will go;*
> *where you lodge, I will lodge;*
> *your people shall be my people,*
> *and your God my God*
> *(Ruth 1:16).*

Harvest time

The two women arrive in Bethlehem. As it is harvest time, Ruth offers to go and gather grain in the fields. Custom allows the poor and the stranger to collect whatever the reapers leave behind (e.g. Deut 24:19). It is not safe for a woman without male relatives to spend time in the fields, but Ruth is willing to take the risk. By chance, she ends up in the field of Boaz, a relative of her deceased father-in-law. Boaz, impressed by Ruth's loyalty to Naomi, provides her with food, protection and privileges.

When Naomi hears this, her strategic skills spring into action. Surviving on gleaned grain will only work during harvest time; a more durable solution needs to be found, and possibly before winter. The only way to achieve permanent protection and income is to become part of a respectable local family, and the only way to do this is by marriage. So Naomi's plan is to get Boaz to marry Ruth.

THE NEXT-OF-KIN AS REDEEMER

The story of Ruth's marriage to Boaz plays on two ancient institutions that are meant to help keep land within the family and maintain family lineage – two central concerns of Israel's agrarian society.

REDEEMER: 'If anyone of your kin falls into difficulty and sells a piece of property, then the next of kin shall come and redeem what the relative has sold' (Lev 25:25). The closest male relative would act as the 'redeemer' and buy the land in question, or buy it back from a third party as soon as possible. If a family member risked being sold into slavery because of debts, the redeemer would pay the price to free them.

LEVIRATE MARRIAGE: If a married man died childless, his brother could be required to marry the widow. The first son of this marriage would then be considered the son of the deceased and inherit his property and land (Deut 25:5-6). This is the background of the dispute in Matt 22:23-33.

The book of Ruth is unique in combining these two institutions, by linking the redemption of Elimelech's land to marrying his widowed daughter-in-law. In doing so, the story creatively ensures security for Naomi and Ruth and the continuity of Naomi's family lineage.

Above: Map showing Ruth's journey between Moab and Bethlehem

Opposite page: Wedding of Ruth and Boaz, by Leopold Bruckner in St Nicholas church, Trnava

> **THE BOOK OF RUTH**
> Although the beginning and ending of the book clearly situates the story in the time of the Judges – before the time of the Monarchy – the story was not written then. While there are many diverging ideas, most biblical scholars today assume a date in the Persian Period (fifth century BCE or later). This makes the book of Ruth comparable to a historical novel set in Shakespeare's time, but written just a few years ago. In fact, the book of Ruth has been described as a 'novella' (small novel), or 'short story'. In this it is similar to the books of Esther, Judith and Tobit, and to the Joseph story in Genesis.

Naomi's plan

Naomi's strategy is unconventional: Ruth is to visit Boaz at night when he sleeps out on a threshing floor. The plan risks Ruth's life and safety, and her reputation would be ruined forever if anyone saw her. Ruth, aware of that but not easily scared, follows her mother-in-law's instructions without question, but with one modification. Naomi tells her to 'uncover his feet and lie down; and he will tell you what to do' (3:4). Ruth, however, waits hidden until Boaz is asleep before she approaches him. Once he wakes up, she immediately asks him to marry her (3:7–9). Though she respectfully calls herself 'your servant', she reminds Boaz that he is next-of-kin and therefore has a responsibility towards her. She thus requests him to treat her with honour, despite the situation, which is deliberately replete with erotic connotations. The combination of both seems to work on Boaz: he swears to marry Ruth, except for one problem – another relative with more direct claims.

But Boaz is determined and solves the problem the next morning; the unnamed relative relinquishes his claims. Boaz marries Ruth with the approval of the entire town. Given that Ruth is a foreigner without any means, this is quite remarkable.

Ruth's and Naomi's new family

Even more remarkable is the reaction of the townswomen to the birth of Ruth's son some time later. They acclaim that, 'A son has been born to Naomi!' (4:16) – not to Boaz, or Ruth. Naomi, who once lost everything, has now regained a family, descendants, her social status, and her peace.

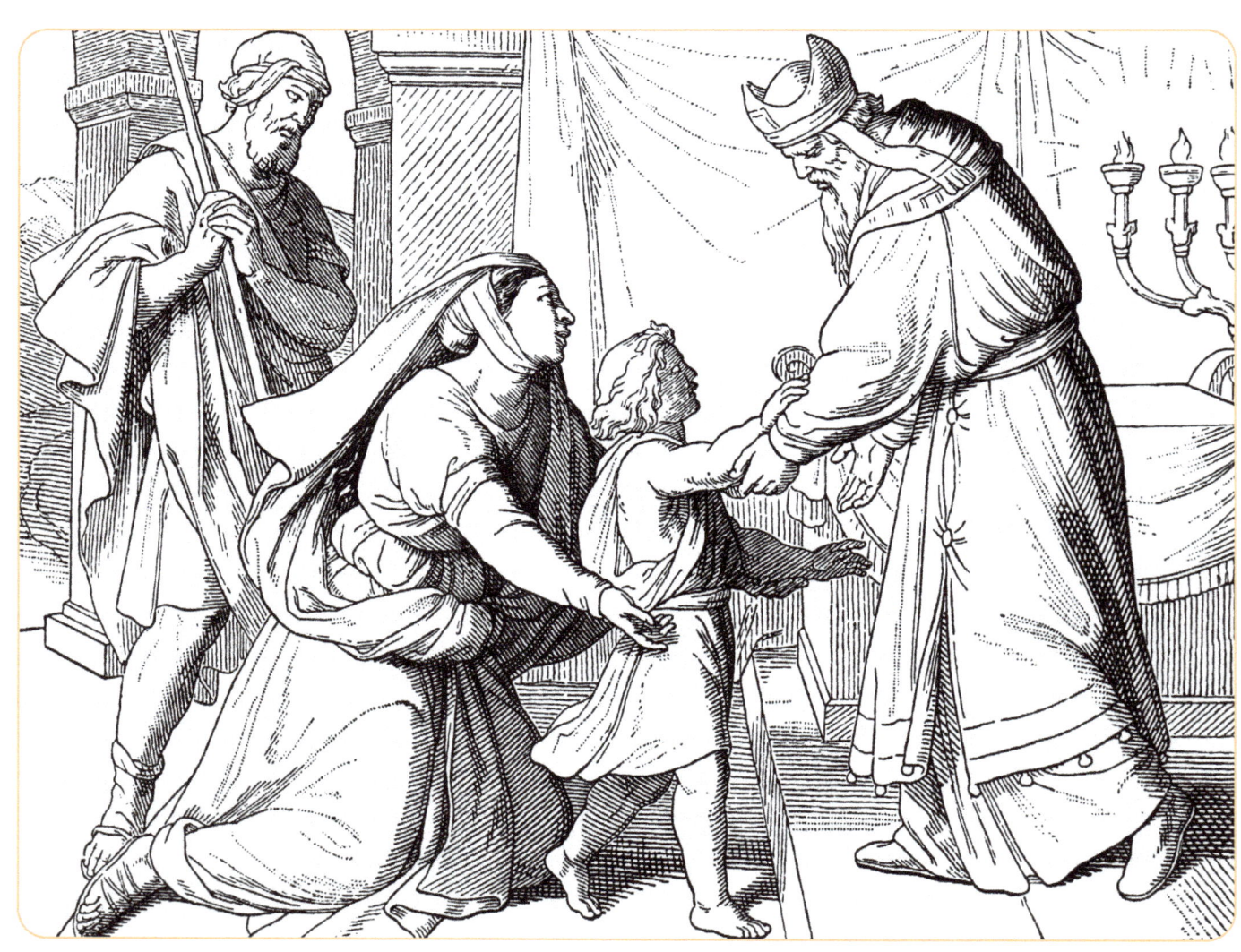

The ending of the story holds yet another surprise: Ruth, the impoverished Moabite widow who used dubious means to find a new husband in Judah, is revealed as the great-grandmother of no other than King David! Ruth's courage and loyalty become part of Israel's history and, in Matthew's gospel, of Jesus's family tree (Matt 1:5).

HANNAH (1 Sam 1:1 – 2:21)

Hannah and her family live in Ramathaim in Ephraim, which, a few generations later, will be part of the kingdom of Israel. But in Hannah's time, Israel has no king yet. Hannah's husband Elkanah is wealthy and he loves her, but Hannah cannot conceive. To ensure the family's future, Elkanah marries a second wife: Peninnah. The years pass and Peninnah has children; Hannah still does not.

Every year, Hannah's family visit the shrine of Shiloh to worship and offer sacrifice. Hannah has dreaded this pilgrimage for many years now. Sacrifices and sacrificial meals are a public affair, and many families gather around the sanctuary. Every year, Peninnah finds ways to draw everyone's attention to Hannah's childlessness and humiliate her. Year after year, Hannah's distress increases until one day, she has had enough. She takes matters to the only one who can help her: she turns to God.

Hannah's prayer comes from a place of deep distress, shame, and anger; crying, she pours out her soul to God. Hannah prays for a child and she adds a vow to her plea: if God grants her a son, she will dedicate him to God 'as a nazirite until the day of his death' (1:11). The nazirite vow was usually temporary; it included abstinence from alcohol and not having one's hair cut.

The power of prayer

Hannah is a changed woman from that moment. When Eli the priest accuses her of drunkenness – yet another attack on her honour and self-esteem – she politely but firmly defends herself (1:14–17). When she returns to her family she joins the celebrations and is 'sad no longer' (1:18).

A short time later, God does 'remember' Hannah (1:19) and she gives birth to a son. She gives him the name Samuel (1:20). When the time seems right to her, Hannah takes Samuel to Shiloh and leaves him under Eli's care (1:24–28) to have him brought up as a servant of God. Every year, Hannah returns to Shiloh to check on her son's welfare and to take him new clothes (2:19). In time, Hannah has another three sons and two daughters (2:21).

Hannah's Song (1 Sam 2:1–10)

As Hannah fulfils her vow she prays again, breaking into a song of praise, which many centuries later inspires the song of Mary, known as the Magnificat (Luke 1:46–55). Both Hannah and Mary celebrate the change that God has worked in their lives and in the lives of many others. In Luke, Mary's praise foreshadows the role and ministry of Jesus. Hannah's song prophetically foreshadows the Davidic monarchy, as Samuel will play a decisive role in its institution.

Hannah's song is a beautiful work of poetry in praise of a mighty God who is deeply concerned for the 'hungry', the 'barren', the 'poor' and the 'needy,' raising them up over those who 'talk so very proudly'.

> Year after year, Hannah's distress increases until one day, she has had enough. She takes matters to the only one who can help her: she turns to God.

HANNAH AND OTHER 'BARREN MOTHERS'

Hannah's story is similar to a number of biblical stories about women who bear a son despite being considered barren, e.g. Sarah, Rachel, Samson's mother (Judg 13:2–25), and Elizabeth in Luke's gospel (Lk 1:5–25). These 'barren mother' stories have strong similarities, not least that the sons are all destined to be decisive figures in Israel's history.

On the one hand, Hannah's story is typical as it follows the common pattern:

- Hannah has no children (1 Sam 1:2).
- Like Sarah and Rachel, Hannah is in rivalry with a second wife who has children (1:4-7).
- By divine intervention (1:19), in which a promise plays a role (1:11), a son is conceived and born (1:20).
- Like Samson and John, Samuel is to be dedicated to God from birth (1:11, 22).

On the other hand, Hannah's story is also unique. Only Hannah takes the initiative in turning directly to God. Only Hannah makes a vow. Usually, when a promise occurs in this type of story, it is a promise that God makes to the woman or her husband, not the other way round.

Opposite page: Hannah presenting her son Samuel to Eli

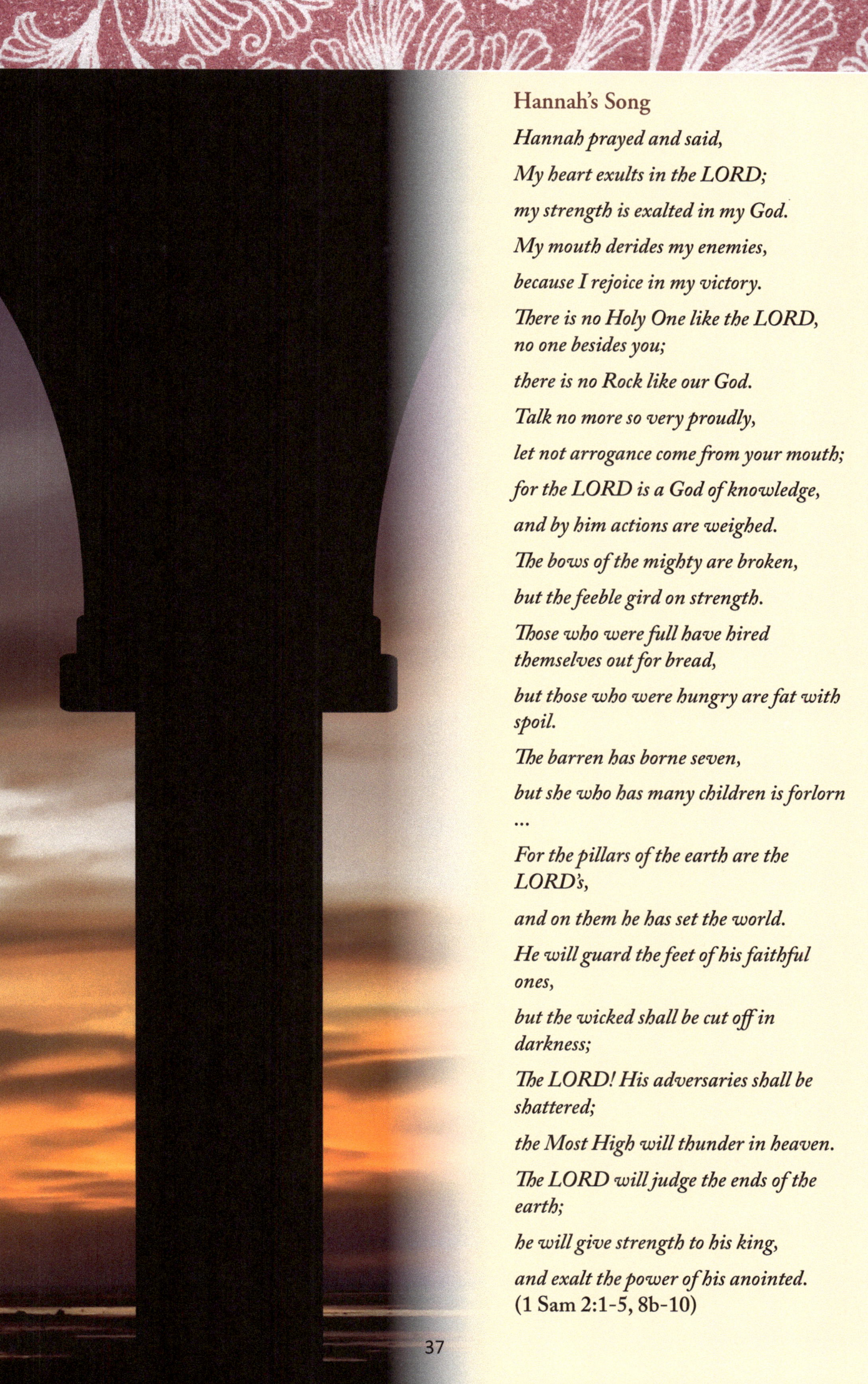

Hannah's Song

Hannah prayed and said,

My heart exults in the LORD;

my strength is exalted in my God.

My mouth derides my enemies,

because I rejoice in my victory.

There is no Holy One like the LORD,
no one besides you;

there is no Rock like our God.

Talk no more so very proudly,

let not arrogance come from your mouth;

for the LORD is a God of knowledge,

and by him actions are weighed.

The bows of the mighty are broken,

but the feeble gird on strength.

Those who were full have hired themselves out for bread,

but those who were hungry are fat with spoil.

The barren has borne seven,

but she who has many children is forlorn ...

For the pillars of the earth are the LORD's,

and on them he has set the world.

He will guard the feet of his faithful ones,

but the wicked shall be cut off in darkness;

The LORD! His adversaries shall be shattered;

the Most High will thunder in heaven.

The LORD will judge the ends of the earth;

he will give strength to his king,

and exalt the power of his anointed.
(1 Sam 2:1-5, 8b-10)

FAMOUS QUEENS

In chess, a pawn can turn into a queen. In real life at court a queen, and especially a princess, could turn into a pawn in political power games. Some queens took the game into their own hands instead.

Israel's monarchy was established roughly around 1000 BCE. The first king, Saul, failed to establish a dynasty. David took his place and united the twelve tribes of Israel into one kingdom, establishing a dynasty that would last for some 400 years. After the death of David's son and successor Solomon, however, the kingdom split into two: Israel in the north (ten tribes), with a number of dynasties supplanting each other; and Judah in the south (the tribes of Judah and Benjamin), under the Davidic dynasty.

MICHAL
(1 Samuel 18–19; 2 Sam 3:13–16; 6:16–22)

Michal is the younger daughter of Ahinoam and Saul, Israel's first king. She is the first woman in Israel's history whose life is totally tangled up in royal politics. As a teenager, Michal falls in love with war hero David. As David marries her, Michal is caught in the middle of an escalating conflict between her husband and her father. Michal saves David's life by helping him escape from Saul (1 Sam 19:11–17). But when David is forced into hiding for several years, Saul asserts his power by giving Michal in marriage to another man. Just when she has settled into her new life, David gains the upper hand. As he reasserts his claim to the throne, Saul's daughter is useful to him and he wants her back. This time Michal has not chosen David; she is forced to return to him. He also has several other wives by then.

The only other incident narrated about Michal (2 Sam 6:16–22) shows her and David exchanging some very sharp and sarcastic remarks. The narrator chooses this point to inform us that Michal never had children. Perhaps she and David never reconciled. Whether due to their discord or brought about by divine will, Michal's childlessness is politically convenient: it ensures that no descendant of Saul will be part of David's dynasty.

ABIGAIL
(1 Samuel 25)

David encounters Abigail at a time when he is fleeing from Saul. Abigail is as pretty as she is clever, but her wealthy husband unfortunately lacks both manners and wits. His name Nabal means 'Fool' in Hebrew. He insults David's men as they politely ask him for provisions. David is furious and already on his way to ravage the whole estate when Abigail hears of the incident. Without breathing a word to her husband she gives orders to assemble enough food to feed an army. With her servants and donkey-loads of tasty presents, she rushes to intercept David. Her food and her wise words transform his anger at her husband into admiration of her 'good sense'. No blood is shed that day.

Life at court for women and men was very different from life in the villages and small towns. Having servants, including 'cooks and bakers' (1 Sam 8:13) meant that the daily workload of women was less heavy. Women at court did not have to fear famine the way villagers did and generally enjoyed a better diet, but illness and infections nevertheless were a threat, especially to young children and women in childbirth. As a status symbol, and to ensure a successor, kings had many wives and secondary wives (concubines). Royal daughters were seen primarily as a potential for forging or reinforcing alliances through their marriage. International marriages must have been very disruptive for a young bride who had to leave not only her family but also her country. As the main wife of the king, a queen would live in a separate quarter of the palace or sometimes have her own palace. Queens had their own estates to manage and their own staff over whom they exercised authority. A queen, and even more a queen mother, could have considerable influence on political, economic and religious decisions; some were the second most powerful person in the kingdom.

Opposite page: Queen of Sheba from the Bellifortis manuscript

Left: Site of ancient ruins that is generally attributed to the location of the Queen of Sheba's palace in Ethiopia

When Nabal realises what almost happened he has a stroke and dies shortly afterwards. David wastes no time in asking Abigail to marry him. As a widow, Abigail is independent so David's messengers address her directly, not a male relative. Abigail accepts immediately. Perhaps, if David had made her his advisor as well as his wife, much more bloodshed could have been avoided.

BATHSHEBA (2 SAMUEL 11–12; 1 KINGS 1–2)

The way Bathsheba became David's wife is possibly the best-known scandal in the Old Testament. Who is she? When David asks that question, he is told, 'Bathsheba daughter of Eliam, the wife of Uriah the Hittite' (2 Sam 11:3). Both men mentioned are among David's trusted warriors of his fighting days (2 Sam 23:24–39).

Much has been speculated about whether Bathsheba knew what she was doing when she bathed within sight of the king's rooftop. Books, paintings and films tend to portray her as seductress but the biblical text does not say this. It only states that David sent for her and slept with her, despite her being married to a man loyal to him. The affair only ends in marriage (and murder) because Bathsheba becomes pregnant and David cannot pass the child off as Uriah's. None of Bathsheba's thoughts or feelings are revealed, except that she grieves about her son who dies as an infant (2 Sam 12:24). The result of David's 'consoling' her is another son: Solomon.

Despite her passive role in the first part of her story, Bathsheba acquires mastery in the power games at court. Her son is way down the list of possible successors to the throne. Nonetheless, Bathsheba and the prophet-in-residence Nathan have enough personal influence on King David, who now is an old man, to ensure that Solomon will be king (1 Kings 1). Nathan's visit to the king's private room has to be formally announced; Bathsheba's standing is such that she can just walk in and, with some gestures of respect, make her request.

Her status as queen mother is even higher. As she approaches Solomon with a request on behalf of his half-brother Adonijah, the king rises from his seat when she enters and bows down to her. Solomon has a throne set up for his mother to sit on his right (1 Kings 2:19). Bathsheba is first in the line of powerful queen mothers

40

at Jerusalem's court. The records of later Judean kings always include the name of the queen mother.

THE QUEEN OF SHEBA
(1 Kings 10:1–13)

The Queen of Sheba differs from other queens in this chapter. First, she is only referred to as 'queen of Sheba', without a personal name. Secondly, she is a foreign queen from a distant country. Sheba, or Saba, is a tribe or kingdom on the Arabian Peninsula (modern Yemen).e There are other traditions, particularly in Ethiopia, that link Sheba to Cush (Ethiopia). In any case, the queen comes to visit Solomon from a faraway wealthy trading empire. As Matthew's gospel puts it, 'she came from the ends of the earth to listen to the wisdom of Solomon' (Matt 12:42).

As the only woman on a par with Solomon, the Queen of Sheba is herself wise and wealthy. Impressed by Solomon's splendour and wisdom, she tests him with riddles and carefully observes his court. They exchange rich gifts – gold, spices and precious stones – before she returns to her country.

The historical basis of this episode probably lies in trading connections Solomon was keen to establish. The story itself is legendary; the royal visit is described in luxurious detail to fill readers with the same awe expressed by the queen. It does so effectively, as it has continually inspired traditions, legends, and artwork and films.

Bathsheba is first in the line of powerful queen mothers at Jerusalem's court. The records of later Judean kings always include the name of the queen mother.

Above: The Queen of Sheba and King Solomon, Gates of Paradise, Florence

Opposite page: Bathsheba receiving David's letter by Rembrandt

JEZEBEL
(1 Kings 16–19; 21; 2 Kings 9)

Jezebel is a Phoenician princess from Sidon, a major port in modern Lebanon. She becomes the wife of the Israelite king Ahab in the ninth century BCE. The kingdom of Israel had broken off from the kingdom of Judah several decades earlier. Her marriage to Ahab surely was motivated by their parents' politics, but Jezebel quickly asserts herself as ambitious, clever and unscrupulous. Ahab's and Jezebel's promotion of Baal worship sparks fierce conflict with the prophet Elijah. (Historically, the Baal cult was not introduced to Israel by Jezebel, though the book of Kings blames her for that.) This conflict results in a long drought and hundreds of murdered prophets on both sides. Jezebel threatens Elijah's life more than once but she never manages to capture him.

Jezebel also abuses her power in the incident of Naboth's vineyard (1 Kings 21). Ahab wants a vineyard in Jezreel, but the owner, Naboth, refuses to sell. Seeing Ahab disappointed, Jezebel takes matters in hand. She arranges the framing and execution of Naboth on fabricated charges so Ahab can take the vineyard. Jezebel is prepared to kill to show who is in charge.

After Ahab's death in battle, Jezebel continues to exercise great power in the role of queen mother, until about

Thanks be to God?!
It can be disconcerting to hear some of these readings, such as Naboth's vineyard, in a liturgical context. The response 'Thanks be to God' seems inappropriate for stories of injustice and murder. Looking at the bigger picture of salvation history instead, this response may not be entirely wrong. When God chose to become involved in the history of Israel, God did not make this dependent on the moral standards, theological orthodoxy or any other measure of perfection of the Israelite people. God engaged with humankind, and in particular with Israel, with all its faults. Shocking events happen in the history of all nations; Israel and Judah are no exceptions. Despite the glaring flaws of some biblical characters, God has never abandoned God's people but continues to walk with them.

843 BCE, when the revolt of military commander Jehu annihilates Ahab's lineage. Apparently Jehu was anointed by a prophet to 'avenge on Jezebel the blood of my servants the prophets' (2 Kgs 9:7).

Jezebel commands respect in her final moments. Knowing that Jehu is coming to kill her, she wears her make-up and royal headdress and awaits death regally. From her window, Jezebel greets Jehu with biting sarcasm, not fear. Jehu is unimpressed and has her thrown out of the window. Like Naboth, Jezebel suffers an inglorious and shameful death. She does not even receive a burial.

ATHALIAH
(2 KINGS 11)

Athaliah is King Ahab's daughter. It is unclear whether her mother is Jezebel or another wife of Ahab. Athaliah possibly surpasses Jezebel in ambition and ruthlessness. As a young princess, Athaliah is married to Jehoram of Judah and consequently queen in Jerusalem. Not much is said about King Jehoram except that Athaliah is seen as a bad influence on him. After his death, Athaliah's son Ahaziah becomes king of Judah, but he is killed during Jehu's uprising in the north (the same that killed Jezebel). As queen mother, Athaliah quite likely has been in charge of government during her son's absence. Now that he is dead, she sees a way to make this permanent. Ahaziah's children, her grandchildren, are still young; nevertheless, his sons are next in line to be king. In order to seize the throne for herself, Athaliah has all of them killed. Only baby Joash is saved.

Nothing about Athaliah's six-year reign is recorded in the book of Kings. The historians were perhaps reluctant to acknowledge a female regent, and the only Judean ruler not of Davidic descent. Besides, what kind of leadership can be expected from someone who kills their own grandchildren? Ultimately, Athaliah's ruthlessness backfires. When Joash is seven years old, chief priest Jehoiada conspires with the temple guards and ceremonially crowns Joash king; Athaliah is put to death on the same day. Unsurprisingly, no one risks their life to come to her aid.

Left: Queen Jezebel and the prophet Elijah, unknown painter, in Basilica del Carmine, Padua

Below: Athalia and Joash by Jose Aparicio (1770–1838) in Real Academia de Bellas Artes de San Fernando

Historically, the Baal cult was not introduced to Israel by Jezebel, though the book of Kings blames her for that.

WOMEN AND PROPHETS

O f the four women in this chapter, the first two appear within a series of miracle stories about the prophet Elijah and his successor Elisha in the book of Kings. Although they have no names, these women are strong characters, whose hospitality and outspokenness create a relationship of trust and friendship with the prophet. On the other hand, Gomer, wife of the prophet Hosea, does have a name but remains a stereotype. Huldah, finally, was a prophet herself, top advisor to the royal court in Jerusalem.

THE WIDOW OF ZAREPHATH (1 Kings 17)

The encounter between the widow and the prophet Elijah is full of irony. Elijah is hiding from Jezebel, and God sends him to Zarephath, near Sidon – Jezebel's homeland. There is a famine, Elijah has run out of food, and God sends him to a widow – someone least likely to have food to spare.

Multiplication of flour and oil

Although the woman of Zarephath and her son are impoverished when Elijah arrives, she has not lost her dignity. At their first encounter, the widow gives the prophet a good talking-to. In the middle of a severe drought, when many are about to starve, he has the nerve to ask her for food! Hospitality is a central value of Middle Eastern cultures still today; under normal circumstances, the woman would happily offer him a meal. But all she has left is a handful of flour and very little olive oil.

Elijah convinces her to share with him what she believes is her last meal. The Sidonian has a quick tongue but a big heart. Her hospitality extends even to a foreigner who serves a different god. She offers him a spare room to stay in. And the miracle happens, daily and quietly: the flour and oil never run out. There is enough for the three of them: the lady of the house, her son, and the prophet.

A son returns to life

When her son suddenly falls ill and dies, his mother becomes angry again. Following a logic common to her time, she interprets her son's death as a divine punishment. Having a 'man of God' in her house, so her reasoning would have attracted the attention of the (Israelite or Sidonian) deity and brought on this calamity. The widow blames Elijah – but he is also her only hope. As the prophet manages to revive the boy, the mother exclaims: 'Now I know that you are a man of God, and that the word of the LORD in your mouth is truth!' (17:24).

This profession of faith reinforces the contrast between the Sidonian widow and the Sidonian queen, Jezebel. The widow is wiser, more perceptive of God and more generous than the queen. In fact, this outspoken non-Israelite woman becomes a role model for any reader of the book of Kings: she is the one person who authoritatively confirms Elijah's identity as a prophet of the

Below: Reconstruction of old Jerusalem including Huldah gates in the late Second Temple period

Opposite: Elijah and the widow of Zarephath from Cleveland Museum of Art

living God. No wonder Jesus cites this story when he wants his compatriots to look beyond their horizon (Luke 4:25–26).

THE GREAT WOMAN OF SHUNEM
(2 Kgs 4:8–37; 8:1–6)

Elisha, Elijah's successor, is also welcomed by a woman but the situation is very different: Elisha comes to the town of Shunem, in Israel, and is urged (literally: 'seized') by a wealthy ('great') woman to stay for a meal. The great woman of Shunem has a husband, considerable means and a strong character. She convinces her husband to build a room for Elisha to stay whenever he passes through on his travels. Her encounter with the prophet takes place entirely on her initiative. She is generous and hospitable to Elisha because she recognises him as 'a man of God' (4:9).

The prophet seeks to reciprocate her generosity, but the woman politely refuses. Elisha learns that she has no children and announces to her that she will have a son. In contrast to other women in a similar situation the Shunammite's response is unique: 'No my lord, don't lie to me!' The prophet seems to have touched a sore point: possibly she had wanted children (for every cultural, practical and emotional reason), but gave up that hope long ago. To be disappointed again would be too much to bear.

The great woman's son

A son is born to the woman sometime later. He is still a boy when he suffers a sunstroke and dies. Again, his mother's reaction is unusual: Telling no one that her son is dead, she travels as fast she can from Shunem to Mt Carmel, about 25-30 km, where Elisha is. As she once 'seized' him to come for dinner – now she 'seizes' his feet, saying, 'Did I ask my lord for a son? Did I not say, 'Do not mislead me'?' (4:28). In other words: This is *your* responsibility; do something! Seeing her 'bitter distress', Elisha returns with her to Shunem and revives the boy.

Property disputes

Their contact remains, as the Shunammite woman reappears some chapters later. Her husband is not mentioned in this episode; perhaps he has died (he is 'old' already in 4:14). After some time abroad because of a severe drought, the woman and her household return to Shunem. As she finds her property occupied, she proceeds to claim it back at the royal court. Years earlier, she refused Elisha's offer to put in a good word for her at court; it is now her connection to Elisha that prompts the king to grant her appeal immediately. Since inheritance usually is passed from father to son, it is intriguing that the land is referred to as 'hers': not her husband's or her son's.

The great woman of Shunem stands for many competent, independent women. She knows what she wants and how to get it. One would not want to get on the wrong side of her – but there is literally nothing she would not do for the people she cares about.

HULDAH
(2 Kgs 22:14–20)

Unlike the two previous women, the prophet Huldah is mentioned in the official royal records of the kingdom of Judah. She is a historical figure who, like Deborah, shows that not all prophets or advisers to the kings of Judah and Israel were men. In the year 622 BCE, Huldah is consulted by King Josiah about 'the book of the law' that has been found in the temple during renovation works (2 Kgs 22:8).

The book contains laws and regulations regarding worship and social life, and serious threats if these regulations are not kept. Josiah fears for the future of his kingdom, and seeks advice from Huldah, the best-qualified person available. Nothing hints at any surprise at his choice; women prophets were nothing unusual.

Huldah recognises the book as the word of God. She is able to apply its words to her time and circumstances and evaluate the consequences. Huldah then pronounces a further oracle from God, confirming the king's fears of looming disaster. Hers is certainly not an easy job. Huldah can be compared to a skilled consultant whose advice is based on expertise and integrity, not on convenience.

GOMER (Hos 1–3)

Gomer may have been a historical woman who lived in the mid-eighth century BCE in the kingdom of Israel and was married to the prophet Hosea. We know hardly anything about her. She is labelled 'a woman of promiscuity' (1:2) before she is introduced by name: 'Gomer, the daughter of Diblaim' (1:3). 'Promiscuity' ('whoredom' in many translations) refers to extramarital relationships. Perhaps Gomer had a lover. Many biblical scholars have assumed her involvement in a Baal fertility cult. The book of Hosea itself is not very specific; the language of prostitution can denote many kinds of illicit sexual conduct, especially of a woman.

Gomer is also a metaphor. She represents Israel: her infidelity to her husband symbolises Israel's infidelity to their God. As some feminist interpreters have noted, this metaphor is hardly fair because it represents God as a man, and sinfulness as a woman. Israel-as-unfaithful-wife (aka Gomer) is accused of not appreciating God's gifts and of running after other benefactors instead: other gods, political alliances, and international trade connections. Severe punishment is threatened (2:3–13), before relationships are restored (2:19–23). There is no indication that the real-life Gomer suffered any of the maltreatment listed.

It is important to be aware of the different levels operating in the passages about Hosea's wife. Gomer is not simply a 'bad woman'; she stands for all Israel, men and women alike. Hosea's and Gomer's troubled family life is symbolic of the political and economic troubles that were leading to the disintegration of Israel's national and religious identity at the time.

Wanton women metaphors

Gomer is the first in a line of symbolic women in the prophetic literature. In the books of Jeremiah and Ezekiel, Jerusalem/Judah is personified as an unfaithful wife whose transgressions and subsequent violent punishment are described in even more disturbing detail than in Hosea. These texts are shocking because of the level of divinely sanctioned violence in them; they have wrongly been used to condone domestic violence and rape. It is important to keep in mind that these metaphors are not meant to promote violence against women. Rather, the literary device of using the metaphor of one woman's conduct and fate to symbolise that of an entire population can graphically demonstrate the collapse of a society and reflect the horrors of war and conquest. These 'women' remind us of the dangers inherent in taking biblical metaphors literally.

DID YOU KNOW?

- The 'book of the law' is probably an early version of the book of Deuteronomy. The kingdom of Judah fell to the Babylonians under the reign of Josiah's son Zedekiah.

Far left: The prophet Huldah left a lasting impression: a set of gates in the southern wall of Jerusalem are known as the 'Huldah Gates'. Although they have been sealed for centuries, they are still visible today.

Left: Huldah predicts the king's fate, engraving by Carl Schuler, 1850

SYMBOLIC WOMEN

One way to describe an abstract quality is to use a symbol or a literary character that personifies it. In the same way, such a symbolic character can represent a group or an entire nation. This chapter is about the two most prominent female personifications in the Old Testament: *Daughter Zion*, the woman embodying Jerusalem, and *Lady Wisdom*, the female figure closest to God.

DAUGHTER ZION

The figure of 'Daughter Zion' is a personification of Jerusalem. She appears in a number of biblical books, especially in Isaiah and Lamentations. Zion (Jerusalem) is God's favoured daughter, sometimes also portrayed as the mother of the people. As the nation faces invasion, Daughter Zion embodies the suffering caused by war and destruction, which are interpreted as a punishment from God. She laments,

> *Is it nothing to you,*
> *all you who pass by?*
> *Look and see if there is any sorrow*
> *like my sorrow,*
> *which was brought upon me,*
> *which the LORD inflicted on the day*
> *of his fierce anger*
> (Lam 1:12)

However, Daughter Zion also personifies resilience and strength. Though humiliated, wounded and bereft, Zion survives. Eventually, she is consoled, redeemed and restored:

> *Break forth together into singing,*
> *you ruins of Jerusalem;*
> *for the LORD has comforted*
> *his people,*
> *he has redeemed Jerusalem.*
> (Isa 52:9)

> *Sing aloud, O daughter Zion;*
> *shout, O Israel!*
> *Rejoice and exult with all your heart,*
> *O daughter Jerusalem!*
> *The LORD has taken away the*
> *judgments against you,*
> *he has turned away your enemies.*
> (Zeph 3:14–15)

Beyond Jerusalem, Daughter Zion reminds us of the sufferings many women face globally through war and hardship, and of their great resilience, courage and strength.

LADY WISDOM

Women are associated with wisdom, a grammatically feminine word in both Hebrew and Greek. Wisdom – more specifically, divine wisdom – is personified as a woman in the books of Proverbs, Ecclesiasticus (Sirach) and Wisdom of Solomon. These books aim at guiding young men to a morally and economically good life. Personifying wisdom as a woman allows the authors to instil a desire for wisdom on a personal and emotional level that goes deeper than mere studies.

Obviously, Wisdom is not an ordinary woman: she is 'Lady Wisdom'. The only appropriate way of speaking about her seems to be poetry:

> *For she is a breath of*
> *the power of God,*
> *and a pure emanation of the glory*
> *of the Almighty;*
> *therefore nothing defiled gains*
> *entrance into her*
> (Wis 7:25).

Wisdom, God, and Creation

Lady Wisdom is the female figure closest to God in the Old Testament. Although she is a metaphor, Lady Wisdom, too, has her story: She was God's first creation (Prov 8:22; Sir 1:4), and God 'poured her out upon all his works' (Sir 1:9). According to Sirach, Lady Wisdom eventually settled in Jerusalem (Sir 24:10–11). The book of Wisdom has her guiding Israel's history from behind the scenes (Wis 9:18–11:1).

Lady Wisdom counsels kings and rulers (Prov 8:15–16; Wis 6:21; 9:11) but she desires to be close to all humankind. Not only does she help anyone who seeks her (Sir 4:11; Wis 6:12), Lady Wisdom takes the initiative in advertising herself in public places. And Wisdom does not age: even after many centuries, her 'radiant and unfading' beauty (Wis 6:12) still fascinates and inspires readers.

Opposite: Saint Sophia monument, Bulgaria

Above: Daughter Zion paper-cut

> Lady Wisdom is the female figure closest to God in the Old Testament.

Above: Sophia, Personification of Wisdom, statue at Ephesus, Turkey

To you, O people, I call, and my cry is to all that live …
The LORD created me at the beginning of his work,
the first of his acts of long ago.
Ages ago I was set up, at the first, before the beginning of the earth.
When there were no depths I was brought forth,
when there were no springs abounding with water.
Before the mountains had been shaped,
before the hills, I was brought forth …
when he had not yet made earth and fields,
or the world's first bits of soil.
When he established the heavens, I was there,
when he drew a circle on the face of the deep,
when he made firm the skies above,
when he established the fountains of the deep,
when he assigned to the sea its limit,
so that the waters might not transgress his command,
when he marked out the foundations of the earth,
then I was beside him, like a master worker;
and I was daily his delight, rejoicing before him always,
rejoicing in his inhabited world and delighting in the human race.
And now, my children, listen to me: happy are those who keep my ways.
(Prov 8:4, 22–32)

Below: Sapientia, in the Goldener Saal, Augsburg town hall

Opposite: Esther before Ahasuerus, from the window in Notre Dame Cathedral, Dinant, Belgium

WOMAN STRANGE

The book of Proverbs juxtaposes Lady Wisdom with Woman Strange. In contrast to Lady Wisdom, Woman Strange personifies all that can be damaging to leading a good life. She is associated with adultery and represents the dangers of breaking the rules of social order. Being lured into the house of Woman Strange will bring death (Prov 2:16–19; 5:3–5; 7:27), whereas following Lady Wisdom and participating at her banquet will lead to life (Prov 9:1–6).

THE WOMAN OF STRENGTH (Prov 31:10–31)

The book of Proverbs ends with a poem dedicated to yet a third woman: the 'woman of strength' or 'woman of worth' (*'eshet hayil*). This poem is sometimes referred to as the 'ode to a capable wife' – it is obviously written from a male perspective. The woman of strength is clearly married, but she is more than just a capable wife. She is an exemplary woman, an idealised model of how a (wealthy) woman might live daily life according to the values, virtues and teachings offered by Lady Wisdom. She is the female counterpart of the wise man that the book of Proverbs promotes.[f]

DID YOU KNOW?

- In the book of Ecclesiasticus or Sirach (written 200–180 BCE), and subsequently in Rabbinic Judaism, Lady Wisdom is identified with the Torah: following the ways of Wisdom coincides with following God's teachings and laws.

- It was common in antiquity to attribute books to famous historical characters. The *Wisdom of Solomon* (named after the tenth-century king of Israel) was in fact written during the first century BCE by a Jewish scholar who was well acquainted with Greek philosophy.

- The books of Ecclesiasticus and Wisdom of Solomon are part of Roman Catholic and Orthodox editions of the Old Testament, but not of Protestant Old Testament editions and the Hebrew Bible.

WOMEN HEROES

The previous chapters have presented some pretty heroic women already. The two women in this chapter, however, are in a different league altogether. Esther and Judith single-handedly save their entire nation/ethnic group from terrible danger, using nothing but their bravery, their cleverness – and their looks.

ESTHER

The book of Esther is a good read without claims of accurate historicity, though with enough detail to appear authentic. The story is set during the Persian Period, at the Persian court in Susa (modern-day Iran); it is packed with exaggerations, irony, and dramatic twists – not to mention lavish banquets.

The book of Esther exists in two versions. The Hebrew version originates in the fourth century in a Persian Jewish diaspora community. It never mentions God. Divine providence is implied in the 'coincidences' of the plot and through the actions of the protagonists, Esther and Mordecai, who are presented as models for Jews in the diaspora. The longer Greek version of Esther comes from a later time when relations with a pagan (Hellenistic) empire had become tense and conflictual; the cultural and religious distinction of Jewish identity are therefore seen as more important. The Greek additions to the book of Esther include two prayers and frequent references to God.

Queen Vashti and the 'beautiful virgins'

Women characters besides Esther only have brief appearances. Vashti is King Ahasuerus's first wife and queen.

> Esther rises to the challenge and transforms from being a 'trophy queen' into a true leader.

Towards the end of an extended drinking banquet, the king sends for Vashti to show off her beauty to his guests. The queen refuses to come. This assertion of autonomy frightens the king's advisers, as they fear that it will encourage '*all* women' to disrespect their husbands (1:17). The entire scene has satirical qualities. Ahasuerus divorces Vashti on the spot, and now seeks a new queen.

To choose a new queen, '*all* the beautiful virgins' of the kingdom are assembled for a kind of beauty contest. The idea that each of these young women has to spend a night with the king so that he can choose his queen has appalled modern readers. It is one of the many exaggerations in the book. The fact that the author obviously does not see it as problematic underlines how little autonomy young women had in that society.

Esther: From Orphan to Queen

Esther is one of the beautiful young virgins. She is an orphan, adopted by her cousin Mordecai. Being Jewish, a member of an ethnic minority, Esther is one of the most vulnerable among the already powerless young women. Yet she is the one chosen to become queen.

Initially, Esther is docile and obedient. She quickly adapts to her

Below: Esther before Ahasuerus by Filippino Lippi, 1478 – 1480

ESTHER IN HINDSIGHT

At the time of its writing, Esther's story was only imagining the dangers that could arise for an ethnic or religious minority. The Hebrew version of Esther was written during the relatively benevolent Persian rule. The first serious persecution of Jewish faith practices and people occurred under a Hellenistic ruler in the 2nd century BCE. The authors of the book of Esther could not have known of the many cruel and bloody pogroms (massacres) against Jewish people occurring again and again in many European nations centuries later. They could not have known of the Holocaust. But we who are reading Esther's story now, know and must never forget that these horrors occurred. Against this background, the biblical book of Esther remains a warning against the ever-present tendency in human societies to marginalise minorities, or to use violence against those who are deemed 'different'.

Opposite: Judith by August Riedel 1840

---

new life and wins everybody's favour. Following Mordecai's instructions, Esther conceals her Jewish identity. Only in the Greek version does Esther show inner resistance to the pagan environment.

More than just a pretty face

The turning point in Esther's character comes in response to a crisis. A decree orders the execution of *all* Jews in the Persian empire on a precise day. Mordecai asks Esther to use her position to intervene. Initially, Esther is reluctant: appearing unsummoned before the king means risking her life. Mordecai reminds her that her life is in danger already and adds, 'Who knows? Perhaps you have come to royal dignity for just such a time as this' (4:14). At that, Esther rises to the challenge and transforms from being a 'trophy queen' into a true leader.

The Greek edition includes a prayer here that shows Esther's trust in God but also her fear. She prays for courage and for the right words to say to the king. When Esther appears before Ahasuerus, she is so anxious that she faints (15:7–15 Greek).

In the Hebrew edition, Esther shows no fear. She knows the king is fond of her beauty and that he tends to make emotion-based decisions. So she dons all her royal attire and Ahasuerus receives her favourably. Instead of approaching the topic directly, Esther invites the king to dinner. Twice. Only at the second banquet Esther puts her petition to the king:

> *'If I have won your favour, O king, and if it pleases the king, let my life be given me – that is my petition – and the lives of my people – that is my request' (7:3).*

Ahasuerus, who did not know about Esther's Jewish heritage, is appalled. The person responsible for the edict is executed and a second edict is made to deter the planned massacre.

Similar to fairy tales, the book of Esther ends with a complete role reversal: On the established day, all those who planned harm for the Jewish community perish instead. Here, too, exaggeration is at work. The following celebrations are then instituted by Queen Esther as the festival of Purim, to be celebrated yearly henceforth.

JUDITH

While the superhero comic genre apparently dates back to the 1930s, tales, myths and legends about heroes with special powers have been around far longer than that. Judith, in the Old Testament book of the same name, may be described as a superhero, though a highly unconventional one.

The context

The book of Judith is clearly fictional. It mixes historical characters from different centuries, and freely invents other characters and places. In Chapter 2, 'Nebuchadnezzar king of the Assyrians' sends out his general Holofernes to conquer all the nations west of Nineveh. Historically, Nebuchadnezzar was the Babylonian king who destroyed Jerusalem in 587 BCE; Holofernes was a Persian general about 200 years later; and Nineveh was the Assyrian capital, destroyed in 612 BCE. This tells us two things: the book of Judith is one of the more recent books in the Old Testament; and it draws creatively on older traditions.

As the story continues, Holofernes destroys city after city and temple after temple. Finally, he arrives at Israel's borders and besieges the town of Bethulia, a fictional place in a strategic position: if Holofernes captures Bethulia, he will have access to the rest of the country. As the people in Bethulia are running out of water they set God an ultimatum: if God does not save them within five days, they will surrender. Time for a superhero.

Judith's 'superpowers'

Judith is a childless widow in Bethulia. Instead of being poor and marginalised, however, she owns 'gold and silver, men and women slaves, livestock, and fields' (8:7) and is held in high regard by the whole town. Still mourning for her late husband Manasseh, Judith lives a secluded life, wears sackcloth under her widow's attire, and spends much of her time fasting and praying.

When she hears of the ultimatum, Judith first summons the town's leaders and reproaches them. Then she goes into superhero mode. Judith's superpowers differ from those of modern heroes – no flying or invisibility. Nevertheless, Judith's special powers clearly exceed those of the ordinary people around her.

Judith's greatest superpower is that she is a woman! No man would have been able to do what she does. A man would have been recognised as a threat; Judith is underestimated by the men. They see a woman, not a warrior.

Accordingly Holofernes treats Judith with courtesy, planning to seduce her, but he drinks too much. Finally alone with Judith,

JUDITH'S SPECIAL POWERS

- **Total fearlessness**
  Judith fears *no-one* but God. Her plan is risky and could have easily seen her killed or raped but she never shows fear.

- **Autonomy**
  Judith is a woman in a male-centred and group-oriented society. Yet she has her own money and no family ties. This allows her to leave town and spend four days in the enemy's camp, accompanied only by her maid.

- **Foreknowledge**
  Judith's plan relies heavily on foreseeing what other people are going to do. She gets it right every time.

- **Piety**
  Before she does anything, Judith prays (Judith 9; and again 13:4–5, 7). She only eats kosher food and is steeped in Israel's traditions.

- **Eloquence**
  Judith speaks more than any other woman in the Bible, and she always convinces her audience. Her prayer seems to even convince God. Holofernes accepts Judith's made-up story without question.

- **Beauty**
  For Judith, superhero costume means she will bathe, anoint herself with fragrant oils, do up her hair, wear her best outfit and put on all her jewellery. The result is a stunning appearance that gives her access to the Assyrian camp and to Holofernes.

DID YOU KNOW?

- Esther's Hebrew name is Hadassah, meaning 'Myrtle' (2:7). In multilingual contexts and diaspora settings it was common to have two names.

- Esther is the only book of the Hebrew Bible not found among the Dead Sea Scrolls at Qumran, the library of a Jewish sect in the first century CE. In fact, the book's inclusion in the biblical canon was still disputed at that time.

- Judith is the Queen of Hearts in French playing cards because, in Jdt 8:28, the town official Uzziah states that she speaks 'out of a true heart'. On standard playing cards Judith is unrecognisable; the version on page 62 makes it more evident. This playing card is based on the French suit, by David Bellot.

- Although the biblical text is clear that Holofernes never gets a chance to touch Judith, paintings throughout the centuries portray Judith in a much less dignified manner.

he passes out, never to wake up. Just as David uses a slingshot to bring down Goliath before beheading him with his own sword, Judith uses her looks and her words to bring down Holofernes before beheading him – with his own sword.

Judith and her maid return to Bethulia with Holofernes' head in a bag. When the Assyrians discover their general 'dead, with his head missing' (14:15) they flee in a panic.

Judith's song (Judith 16)

Judith praises the God of Israel for the success of her mission. Her song recalls the song of Miriam in Exodus 15 and the song of Deborah in Judges 5.

> *But the Lord Almighty*
> *has foiled them by the*
> *hand of a woman.*
> *For their mighty one*
> *did not fall by the*
> *hands of the young men,*
> *nor did the sons of the Titans*
> *strike him down,*
> *nor did tall giants set upon him;*
> *but Judith daughter of Merari*
> *with the beauty of her countenance*
> *undid him*
> *…*
> *Her sandal ravished his eyes,*
> *her beauty captivated his mind,*
> *and the sword severed his neck!*
> (Jdt 16:5b-6, 9)

Judith the hero

Judith is a combination of femme fatale and pious wise woman; simultaneously a credible moral authority and a deadly warrior. Transcending all the limits of ordinary life, Judith is no more a model to imitate than Superman or Wonder Woman. Superheroes are popular because they protect the vulnerable and make good triumph over evil. Judith does precisely that: 'No one ever again spread terror among the Israelites during the lifetime of Judith, or for a long time after her death' (16:25).

Right: Judith severing the head of Holofernes, by Cristofano Allori

THEIR STORIES AND THEIR WISDOM FOR TODAY

In reading this volume of the *Friendly Guide* series, you have encountered, at least briefly, some forty women of the Old Testament. I could not write about all women mentioned in the Old Testament; that is why I have listed their names in the following pages.

The women in the Old Testament are as diverse as the men, and indeed as characters in any book and the people you meet in everyday life. Hardly any of these women are perfect; not all their stories are edifying, not all are based on historical facts. Each story, however, was considered important enough to be written down and preserved over more than twenty centuries. For better or worse, all these women have played a role in the great story of God's involvement with humankind that we call the history of salvation. They are part of the cultural and religious heritage Jesus would have grown up with, and of the ancient roots of our own faith, whether Jewish or Christian.

If you wish to deepen the acquaintance and get to know any particular woman character in more depth, the Scripture citations within this book will help you finding each story in the Bible to read for yourself, and you can find suggestions for further reading in the bibliography. Various Study Bibles also provide helpful notes that assist with reading the biblical texts.

Even across the huge gap of time, space and culture, the women in the Old Testament still inspire, teach, and impart their wisdom to readers today.

MORE WOMEN IN THE OLD TESTAMENT

Cain's wife (Gen 4:17) Adah and Zillah, wives of Lamech (Gen 4:19-23) Naamah, daughter of Lamech and Zillah (Gen 4:22) The "daughters of humans" taken as wives by the "sons of god" (Gen 6:1-4) Noah's wife and the wives of his sons (Gen 7:7) Lot's wife and their two daughters (Gen 19) Keturah, Abraham's wife after Sarah's death (Gen 25:1) Deborah, Rebekah's nurse (Gen 35:8) Timna, mother of Amalek (Gen 36:12) Mehetabel, wife of Hadar king of Edom, and Matred, her mother (Gen 36:39) Judah's wife, the daughter of Shua (Gen 38:2) Tamar, Judah's daughter-in-law and mother of his sons Perez and Zerah (Gen 38:6-30) Potiphar's wife who tries to seduce Joseph (Gen 39:7-19) Asenath, Joseph's Egyptian wife, mother of Manasseh and Ephraim (Gen 41:50) Serah, daughter of Asher, granddaughter of Jacob (Gen 46:17) Ephraim's wife and Sheerah, their daughter (1 Chr 7:23-24) Elisheba, wife of Aaron (Exod 6:23) Wife of Aaron's son Eleazar, mother of Phinehas (Exod 6:25) Shelomith, daughter of Dibri. Her son was stoned for blasphemy (Lev 24:11) Moses's Cushite wife (Num 12:1) Moabite women who had sexual relationships with Israelites (Num 25:1) Cozbi, a Midianite woman. Her relationship with an Israelite man was seen as the cause of a plague. Both were killed. (Num 25:6-18) More Midianite women are killed in Num 31. Maacah, wife of Machir (1 Chr 7:16) Mahlah, Noah, Hoglah, Milcah, and Tirzah, daughters of Zelophehad, create a legal precedence for inheriting their deceased father's possessions (Num 27:1-8). Azubah, Jerioth and Ephrath, Caleb's wives (1 Chr 2:18-19) Ephah and Maacah, Caleb's concubines (1 Chr 2:46, 48) Achsah, Caleb's daughter, negotiates her dowry (Josh 15:16-19). Abijah, wife of Hezron (1 Chr 2:23) Atarah, wife of Jerahmeel (1 Chr 2:26) Abihail, wife of Abishur (1 Chr 2:29) Sheshan's daughter, wife of Jarha (1 Chr 2:35) Hazzelelponi, daughter of Etam (1 Chr 4:3) Helah and Naarah, wives of Ashhur (1 Chr 4:5) Bithiah, daughter of Pharaoh, wife of Mered (1 Chr 4:16) Hodiah's wife, the sister of Naham (1 Chr 4:19) Shimei's six daughters (1 Chr 4:27) Shua, daughter of Heber (1Chr 7:32) Hushim, Baara and Hodesh, wives of Shaharaim (1 Chr 8:8-9) Maacah, wife of Jeiel (1 Chr 8:29) The wives and concubines of Gideon (Judg 8:30-31) The woman who "threw an upper millstone on Abimelech's head, and crushed his skull" (Judg 9:53) Gilead's wife, and the prostitute who was the mother of Gilead's son Jephthah (Judg 11:1-2) Jephthah's daughter (Judg 11:34-40) Thirty daughters and thirty daughters-in-law of Ibzan of Bethlehem (Judg 12:9) Manoah's wife, the mother of Samson (Judg 13) Micah's mother (Judg 17:2-4) The Levite's concubine (Judges 19) 400 virgins from Jabesh-gilead, abducted to be wives for the Benjaminites (other townswomen are killed) Young women of Shiloh, abducted for the same purpose (Judg 21:8-23) Eli's daughter-in-law (1 Sam 4:19-22) Zeruiah and Abigail, David's sisters (1 Chr 2:16) Merab, daughter of Saul, Michal's older sister (1 Sam 14:49) Ahinoam, wife of King Saul, mother of Michal (1 Sam 14:50) Women singing in praise of David (1 Sam 18:6-7) Ahinoam of Jezreel, one of David's wives, mother of Amnon (1 Sam 25:43) Haggith, Maacah, Abital and Eglah, also David's wives (2 Sam 3:4-5) Medium of Endor (1 Sam 28:7-25) Rizpah, King Saul's concubine (2 Sam 21:10) The wise woman from Tekoa (2 Sam 14:2-20) Tamar, Absalom's daughter (so named after his sister) (2 Sam 14:27) Ten of King David's concubines, raped by Absalom (2 Sam 15:16) A servant-girl and a woman who help David's men against Absalom (2 Sam 17:17-20) Zeruiah, mother of David's general Joab, and her sister Abigal (2 Sam 17:25) The wise woman from Abel Beth-maacah (2 Sam 20:16-22) Abishag the Shunammite, personal attendant of the aged King David (1 Kgs 1:3-4) Daughter of Pharaoh, Solomon's main wife (1 Kgs 3:1) Solomon's 700 other wives and 300 concubines (1 Kgs 11:3) Two prostitutes who argue about the identity of a baby (1 Kgs 3:16-28) Taphath and Basemath, Solomon's daughters (1 Kgs 4:11+15) Tahpenes, Queen of Egypt, and her sister, wife of Hamad (1 Kgs 11:19) Zeruah, mother of King Jeroboam I (1 Kgs 11:25) King Jeroboam's wife (1 Kgs 14:2-4) Naamah, mother of King Rehoboam (1 Kgs 14:21) Mahalath, granddaughter of David, first wife of King Rehoboam (2 Chr 11:18) Abihail, mother of Mahalath (1 Chr 11:18) Maacah, favourite wife of Rehoboam, mother of Kings Abijah and Asa (2 Chr 11:20-21) Rehoboam's sixteen other wives, sixty concubines, and sixty daughters (2 Chr 11:21) Azubah, mother of King Jehoshaphat (1 Kgs 22:42) The widow of a prophet, follower of Elisha (2 Kgs 4:1-7) The Israelite servant-girl of Naaman's wife (2 Kgs 5:2-3) Two cannibal mothers (2 Kgs 6:26-29) Jehosheba, King Joram's daughter (2 Kgs 11:2) Zibiah, mother of King Jehoash (2 Kgs 12:1) Jehoaddin, mother of King Amaziah (2 Kgs 14:2) Jecoliah, mother of King Azariah/Uzziah (2 Kgs 15:2) Jerusha, mother of King Jotham (2 Kgs 15:33) Abijah, mother of King Hezekiah (2 Kgs 18:2) Hephzibah, mother of King Manasseh (2 Kgs 21:1) Meshullemeth, mother of King Amon (2 Kgs 21:19) Jedidah, mother of King Josiah (2 Kgs 22:1) Hamutal, mother of Kings Jehoahaz and Zedekiah (2 Kgs 23:31; 24:18) Zebidah, mother of King Jehoiakim (2 Kgs 23:36) Nehushta, mother of King Jehoiachin, exiled to Babylon (2 Kgs 24:8) Shelomith, daughter of Zerubbabel (1 Chr 3:19) The foreign women whose marriages with Judeans were annulled by Ezra (Ezra 9-10) Shallum's daughters (Neh 3:12) Noadiah, the prophetess (Neh 6:14) Zeresh, wife of Haman (Est 5:10) Job's three daughters before his trial (Job 1:2) Job's wife (Job 2:9-10) Jemimah, Keziah and Keren-Happuch, Job's daughters after his trial (Job 42:14) Mother of King Lemuel who taught him (Prov 31) The young woman in the Song of Solomon The prophetess, Isaiah's wife (Isa 8:3) The young woman who will bear a son and name him Immanuel (Isa 7:14) False prophetesses (Ezek 13:17-23) Ezekiel's wife (Ezek 24:16-18) Lo-ruhama, daughter of Hosea and Gomer "Wickedness" in the basket and two winged women in Zechariah's vision (Zech 5:5-11) Deborah, grandmother of Tobit (Tob 1:8) Anna, Tobit's wife, mother of Tobias (Tob 2:11-14) Sarah, daughter of Raguel, wife of Tobias (Tob 3) Edna, wife of Raguel, mother of Sarah (Tob 7)

MORE WOMEN IN THE OLD TESTAMENT

BIBLIOGRAPHY

Ackerman, Susan. *Warrior, Dancer, Seductress, Queen: Women in Judges and Biblical Israel.* New Haven, CT: Yale University Press, 1998.

Bergant, Dianne. *Genesis: In the Beginning.* Collegeville, MN: Liturgical Press, 2013.

Branch, Robin Gallaher. 'Judith: A Remarkable Heroine.' Part 1. Biblical Archaeological Society. Last modified 31 January 2020. https://www.biblicalarchaeology.org/daily/people-cultures-in-the-bible/people-in-the-bible/judith-a-remarkable-heroine/

——— . 'Judith: A Remarkable Heroine.' Part 2. Biblical Archaeological Society. Last modified 1 February 2020. https://www.biblicalarchaeology.org/daily/people-cultures-in-the-bible/people-in-the-bible/judith-a-remarkable-heroine-part-2/

Camp, Claudia V. '1 and 2 Kings.' In *The Women's Bible Commentary,* edited by Carol A. Newsom and Sharon H. Ringe, 96–109. Louisville, KY: Westminster John Knox, 1992.

Cook, Joan E. *Hannah's Desire, God's Design: Early Interpretations of the Story of Hannah.* London: Bloomsbury, 1999. ProQuest Ebook Central. Accessed December 6, 2020.

Crawford, Sidnie White. 'Esther.' In *The Women's Bible Commentary,* edited by Carol A. Newsom and Sharon H. Ringe, 124–29. Louisville, KY: Westminster John Knox, 1992.

Ebeling, Jennie R., *Women's Lives in Biblical Times.* London; New York: T&T Clark, 2010.

Esler, Phillip F. *Sex, Wives, and Warriors: Reading Old Testament Narrative with Its Ancient Audience.* Cambridge: Lutterworth Press, 2011. doi:10.2307/j.ctt1cgf12k.7.

Exum, J. Cheryl. *Plotted, Shot, and Painted: Cultural Representation of Biblical Women.* 2nd ed. Sheffield: Sheffield Phoenix Press, 2012.

Fox, Michael V. *Proverbs 10–31.* Anchor Yale Bible 18B. New Haven: Yale University Press, 2009.

Fretheim, Terence E. *Exodus.* Interpretation: A Bible Commentary for Teaching and Preaching. Louisville, KY: Westminster John Knox Press, 2010.

Frymer-Kensky, Tikva. *Reading the Women of the Bible.* New York: Schocken Books, 2002.

Galpaz-Feller, Pnina. 'The Widow in the Bible and in Ancient Egypt.' ZAW 120, no. 2 (2008): 231–53. doi:10.1515/ZAW.2008.014.

Gera, Deborah Levine. *Judith.* Commentaries on Early Jewish Literature. Boston: De Gruyter, 2014.

Hoppe, Leslie. "Images *of Jerusalem in the Hebrew Bible."* Bible Odyssey. Accessed 16 Mar 2021. http://www.bibleodyssey.com/places/related-articles/images-of-jerusalem-in-the-hebrew-bible

Keefe, Alice A. 'Family Metaphors and Social Conflict in Hosea.' In: *Writing and Reading War: Rhetoric, Gender, and Ethics in Biblical and Modern Contexts*, edited by Brad E. Kelle and Frank Ritchel Ames, 113–127. Atlanta, GA: Society of Biblical Literature, 2008.

Kelle, Brad E. 'Hosea 1–3 in Twentieth-Century Scholarship.' *Currents in Biblical Research* 7, no. 2 (2009): 179–216doi:10.1177/1476993X08099542.

Knowles, Melody. "Zion." Bible Odyssey. Accessed 16 Mar 2021. http://www.bibleodyssey.com/places/main-articles/zion

Marsman, Hennie J. *Women in Ugarit and Israel: Their Social and Religious Position in the Context of the Ancient Near East.*

Oudtestamentische Studiën 49. Leiden: Brill, 2003.

Mayfield, Tyler D. 'The Accounts of Deborah (Judges 4–5) in Recent Research.' *Currents in Biblical Research* 7, no. 3 (June 2009): 306–35 doi:10.1177/1476993X09104456.

McCabe, Elizabeth A. 'Answers to Unresolved Questions: A Closer Look at Eve and Adam in Genesis 2-3.' In: *Women in the Biblical World: A Survey of Old and New Testament Perspectives*. Edited by Elizabeth A. McCabe, 1–20. Lanham, MD: UPA, 2009.

Meyers, Carol. *Rediscovering Eve: Ancient Israelite Women in Context*. New York: OUP, 2013.

Morrison, Craig E. *Berit Olam: 2 Samuel*. Collegeville, MN: Liturgical Press, 2013.

Morse, Holly. *Encountering Eve's Afterlives: A New Reception Critical Approach to Genesis 2–4*. Oxford: Oxford University Press, 2020. Oxford Scholarship Online, 2020. doi: 10.1093/oso/9780198842576.001.0001.

Nowell, Irene. *Women in the Old Testament*. Collegeville, MN: Liturgical Press, 2017.

Parker, Julie Faith. 'You Are a Bible Child: Exploring the Lives of Children and Mothers Through the Elisha Cycle.' In *Women in the Biblical World: A Survey of Old and New Testament Perspectives,* edited by Elizabeth A. McCabe, 69–78. Lanham, MD: UPA, 2009.

Quick, Laura. 'The Book of Ruth and the Limits of Proverbial Wisdom.' JBL 139, no. 1 (2020): 47-66.

Schipper, Jeremy. *Ruth: A New Translation with Introduction and Commentary*. AB 7D. New Haven: Yale University Press, 2016.

Schneider, Tammi. 'Who Is Interpreting the Text? A Feminist Jewish Hermeneutic of Deborah.' In *Women in the Biblical World: A Survey of Old and New Testament Perspectives*. Edited by Elizabeth A. McCabe, 23–35. Vol. 2. Lanham, MD: UPA, 2011.

The Harper Collins Study Bible: Fully Revised and Updated. Edited by Harold W. Attridge et al. New York: HarperOne, 2006.

Webster, Jane S. 'Sophia: Engendering Wisdom in Proverbs, Ben Sira and the Wisdom of Solomon.' JSOT 23 (1998): 63–79.

'Art of Susanna and the Elders.' Bible Odyssey. Accessed 5 Jan 2021. https://www.bibleodyssey.org:443/people/related-articles/art-of-susanna-and-the-elders

WiBiLex: Das wissenschaftliche Bibellexikon im Internet. Edited by Deutsche Bibelgesellschaft. https://www.bibelwissenschaft.de/wibilex/das-bibellexikon/

Yoder, Christine Roy. "Woman Wisdom and the Woman of Substance." Bible Odyssey. Accessed 6 Mar 2021. https://www.bibleodyssey.org:443/passages/related-articles/woman-wisdom.

ENDNOTES

[a] Carol Meyers, *Rediscovering Eve: Ancient Israelite Women in Context* (New York: OUP, 2013), 203.

[b] Dianne Bergant, *Genesis: In the Beginning*. (Collegeville, MN: Liturgical Press, 2013), 29.

[c] See Terence E. Fretheim, *Exodus. Interpretation: A Bible Commentary for Teaching and Preaching* (Louisville, KY: Westminster John Knox Press, 2010), 79-81.

[d] Peter Riede, 'Biene,' in: WiBiLex: Das wissenschaftliche Bibellexikon im Internet (2009), https://www.bibelwissenschaft.de/stichwort/15333/.

[e] Peter Stein, 'Saba,' in: WiBiLex: Das wissenschaftliche Bibellexikon im Internet (2014). https://www.bibelwissenschaft.de/stichwort/25250/.

[f] Michael V. Fox, *Proverbs 10–31*. (AB 18B; New Haven: Yale University Press, 2009), 912.

ACKNOWLEDGMENTS

At the conclusion of this *Friendly Guide to Women in the Old Testament* I would like to acknowledge a number of people without whom this volume would not have been completed. The idea for this volume originated from within Garratt Publishing, and I feel privileged to have been approached for its realisation. I thank the team at Garratt Publishing, especially Rose Inserra, for the friendly, enthusiastic and supportive collaboration.

I am grateful to Associate Professor Mark O'Brien OP for agreeing to read a draft version of the manuscript and for offering his very helpful comments, food for thought and support.

Special thanks to Margaret Brown, Vinca Alcantara, Corre Ruse, Lorraine Mascarenhas and everyone in the Focolare community who read portions of the manuscript, helped me in practical ways, and allowed me to share my daily discoveries with them. Your feedback and support have been essential. I hope that this book will spark discussions among its readers that are similar to those we enjoyed during its preparation.

Published in Australia by
Garratt Publishing
32 Glenvale Crescent
Mulgrave, VIC 3170

www.garrattpublishing.com.au

Text copyright © Janina Hiebel 2021

All rights reserved. Except as provided by the Australian copyright law, no part of this book may be reproduced in any way without permission in writing from the publisher.

Design and typesetting by Lynne Muir
Cover Image: Alamy
Images: Alamy p 31
Wikimedia Commons pp 7, 8, 10, 12, 13, 16, 20, 21, 22, 27, 32, 38, 40, 42, 43, 44, 49, 50, 52, 54, 57, 58, 62
iStock pp 1, 4, 9, 18, 20, 25, 28, 34, 36, 39, 41, 45, 47, 48, 50, 53, 59, 63, 64

Rosemary Canavan pp 8, 23, 26 46, Free Bible Society pp 3, 5

Nihil Obstat: Reverend Gerard Diamond MA (Oxon), LSS, D.Theol, Diocesan Censor, Catholic Archdiocese of Melbourne

Imprimatur: Very Reverend Joseph Caddy, AM Lic. Soc. Sci VG, Vicar General, Catholic Archdiocese of Melbourne

Date: 10 June 2021

The Nihil Obstat and Imprimatur are official declarations that a book or pamphlet is free of doctrinal or moral error. No implication is contained therein that those who have granted the Nihil Obstat and Imprimatur agree with the contents, opinions or statements expressed. They do not necessarily signify that the work is approved as a basic text for catechetical instruction.

Scripture quotations are from *New Revised Standard Version Bible: Catholic Edition*, copyright © 1989, 1993 National Council of the Churches of Christ in the United States of America. Used by permission. All rights reserved worldwide.

ISBN 9 781925 009729

Cataloguing in Publication information for this title is available from the National Library of Australia.
www.nla.gov.au

The author and publisher gratefully acknowledge the permission granted to reproduce the copyright material in this book. Every effort has been made to trace copyright holders and to obtain their permission for the use of copyright material. The publisher apologises for any errors or omissions in the above list and would be grateful if notified of any corrections that should be incorporated in future reprints or editions of this book.

www.ingramcontent.com/pod-product-compliance
Lightning Source LLC
Chambersburg PA
CBHW061058170426
43199CB00025B/2933